Hadrian
and his
Wall

Hadrian
and his
Wall

Paul Frodsham

NORTHERN
HERITAGE

First published in the United Kingdom in 2013 by Northern Heritage Publishing.
Reprinted 2017

Northern Heritage
Units 7&8 New Kennels, Blagdon Estate, Seaton Burn,
Newcastle upon Tyne NE13 6DB
Telephone: 01670 789 940
www.northern-heritage.co.uk

See our full online catalogue at www.northern-heritage.co.uk

Printed and bound in Great Britain by Martins the Printers.
Berwick-upon-Tweed

British Library Cataloguing in Publishing Data
A catalogue record for this book is available from the British Library.

ISBN 978-0-9572860-3-0

This book is published in partnership with:

Supported by:

Contents

This book is affectionately and respectfully dedicated to the memory of
PAUL BENIAMS
a good friend of the Wall
who did much to further its enjoyment by others.

Acknowledgements

I am grateful to the many people with whom I have discussed aspects of Hadrian and his Wall over recent years, in particular Rob Young (English Heritage) and Nigel Mills (Hadrian's Wall Trust) who read an early draft of this book and made many helpful comments. Thanks also to Chris Jones and Derek Proudlock of the Northumberland National Park Authority for their support.

Appropriate acknowledgements for illustrations are included within the relevant captions; where no acknowledgement is present, the images are the work of the author. Many of the images are sourced from Wikimedia Commons (www.commons/ wikimedia.org), where it is stated that they are either in the public domain or otherwise freely available for reproduction. In all cases (although apparently unnecessarily, given the terms on which they are made available on Wikimedia) attempts have been made to contact the original photographers to ensure they are correctly acknowledged, and to offer a complementary copy of the book. I am grateful to those who have responded, all of whom have confirmed they are happy for their work to be included. In some cases it has proved impossible to contact the original photographers; in these cases, the acknowledgement is based on information drawn directly from Wikimedia. Further efforts will be made to contact these individuals and should any amendments be necessary then these will be made in future editions. I am most grateful to all the photographers, both for their photographic expertise and their generosity in making their work available through Wikimedia. Particular thanks are due to Marie-Lan Nguyen, many of whose excellent photographs are included.

I am most grateful to Graeme Peacock, one of northern England's most accomplished landscape photographers, for permission to use several of his splendid photographs of the Wall landscape. Thanks also to Sheena Butler (acting on behalf of the trustees of Frank Graham) for consent to include a selection of Ronald Embleton's reproductions of sites along the Wall.

Further help with illustrations was forthcoming from: Chris Sutherns at the British Museum; Javis Gurr at English Heritage; Andrew Parkin at the Great North Museum, Newcastle upon Tyne; Tim Padley at Tullie House Museum, Carlisle; Andrew Birley and Barbara Birley at the Vindolanda Trust; Marc Waelkens and Joeri Theelen of the Sagalassos Archaeological Research Project; Dale Tatro and Travis Markel of the Classical Numismatic Group, Inc.; Bella Gershovich at the The Israel Museum, Jerusalem; Angela Carbonaro and Claudio Parisi Presicce at the Musei Capitolini, Rome. I am grateful to all.

I am also pleased to record my gratitude to Stan Beckensall, Mel Clark (Airfotos

Ltd;), Ian Bracegirdle, Christof Flügel, Clement Kuehn, and Dick Osseman for generously providing their own photographs for inclusion in the book. Thanks also to Rebecca Barrett and Elisabeth Langton-Airey for help with illustrations, proof reading and other stuff.

I would like to take this opportunity to thank my partner, Diane Anderson, and my daughters Katie and Claire, who have been forced to live with Hadrian for far too long, even if they did get to visit some fascinating places, from *Arbeia* to Antalya, *Luguvalium* to Luxor.

I am very grateful to Ian Scott for his design expertise, enabling him to transform a collection of Word files and jpegs into this attractively presented book, and also for his infinite patience as further alterations and corrections were made, on more than one occasion, to the latest version of the 'final' proof. Thanks are also due to Ian for generously providing several of his own splendid photographs of the Wall for inclusion in the book. Finally, and most importantly, I would like to thank Chris Hartnell at Northern Heritage Ltd for his loyal support and patience throughout what has been a rather lengthier project than originally intended.

PF
Weardale
February 2013

Introduction

If we ever imagine we glimpse some new truth about Hadrian's Wall, it is simply because we stand on the shoulders of giants.
                                                                Brian Dobson, 1985.

Not another book about Hadrian's Wall! Yes, but this one, I hope, is rather different from the others. Its origins are rooted in a question that has intrigued me for years: to what extent is 'Hadrian's Wall' actually 'Hadrian's'? The basic structure of the book, rather like that of the Wall, is quite simple. It focuses on Hadrian the man before considering the Wall, then considers the relationship between the two. The illustrations are arranged in two batches: the first includes images of Hadrian and his various architectural projects, the second focuses on the Wall, providing something of a tour along its line from east to west.

This book also differs from most others about the Wall in that it is not the work of a Romanist. I am not, and nor do I ever wish to be regarded as, a Roman specialist. (Romanists, having read what follows, may well consider this no bad thing). Most people who study and write about the Wall are trained in classical archaeology, whereas my background is in landscape archaeology; I like to think that I favour no particular period over any other when seeking to explain changes in the landscape and in human society over the past 10,000 years. That said, I am aware that many colleagues and friends see in me a pathological hatred of all things Roman. The explanation is simple: when I took up the post of Northumberland National Park Archaeologist in 1992 it seemed to me that Roman archaeology (even allowing for the international interest in the Hadrian's Wall World Heritage Site) devoured a disproportionately large slice of the far from substantial financial pie on which all archaeological work in Northumberland depended. As part of my aim to restore the balance I was on occasion less than complimentary about our Roman friends, suggesting that Hadrian's Wall acted as an efficient barrier in precluding the of passage archaeological funds to its north. Now, however, having overseen much work into pre-Roman and post-

Roman archaeology, I find myself increasingly drawn to this remarkable phase of Northumbrian history, and I hope this book will help to demonstrate that my perceived hatred of Romans was never anything other than a publicity stunt in favour of, amongst other things, Neolithic rock art, Iron Age hillforts and medieval castles.

While working on this book, which has taken far too long, I had the good fortune to visit the British Museum's marvellous *Hadrian – Empire & Conflict* exhibition which ran from July to October 2008. This brought Hadrian to the attention of the nation, and was visited by a quarter of a million people, all of whom must have left with a realisation that Rome's fourteenth emperor was a charismatic and complex character who played a key role in the story of the empire. On a personal level, my partner and daughters (who have no great interest in archaeology and thus ensure, to my great advantage, that I occasionally do other things) became understandably weary of being dragged around Roman sites and listening to me droning on about what an amazing character Hadrian must have been. One incident, though, took them somewhat by surprise and left them thinking that maybe I had something of a point. While passing through Newcastle airport one autumn for a half-term break in Turkey, one of my dear daughters was heard to murmur on walking past a huge advertisement for Hadrian's Wall country, 'at least we're leaving that behind for a few days, maybe Dad will talk about something else for a change!' A few hours later, on shuffling half asleep into the arrivals lounge at Antalya airport, what was the very first thing we saw? A statue of Hadrian! I was pleasantly surprised; they were astonished. I seem to recall a muttered 'okay Dad, maybe he was quite an important bloke after all'. The point being that nineteen centuries ago, and without the benefits of modern transport or communications, Hadrian had been familiar with both Northumbria and Turkey, along with most places in between and many further afield. And not only had he been familiar with these places, but for two decades in the early second century he was the undisputed and generally popular ruler of them all. It is in this context that we must try to understand Hadrian's Wall.

The magnificent British Museum exhibition, and associated book by Thorsten Opper, were by no means the only evidence of public interest in Hadrian and his Wall that materialised between my acceptance of the invitation to write this book and its eventual publication. In July 2008, the BBC broadcast an hour-long documentary to tie in with the British Museum exhibition. Entitled simply 'Hadrian' it was watched by 2.2 million viewers. In his introduction, the presenter, Dan Snow, states:

'Hadrian; not only was he one of the greatest of the Roman emperors, but I've always found him one of the most enigmatic and fascinating characters in the whole

of ancient history.......I want to learn about the empire that Hadrian knew, travelled around and dominated more than any other Roman emperor, I want to see the architecture that he commissioned, I want to see the places that inspired him, and above all I want to get to know Hadrian as a man.'

This book has similar aims, but with specific regard to a better understanding of the Wall.

In March 2009, esteemed Wall scholar, David Breeze, gave a well-attended lecture to a joint meeting of the Societies of Antiquaries of Newcastle upon Tyne and of London entitled *Did Hadrian design Hadrian's Wall?* (published later that year – see references). After much stimulating discussion, the conclusion was that he must have been involved in some capacity in the initial design, but that the extent of his detailed involvement in the project remains, and may always remain, unresolved.

August 2009 saw the thirteenth decennial pilgrimage along the Wall. More than 200 'pilgrims' spent a week travelling the length of the Wall, and to places beyond, with on-site lectures, discussions and events provided along the way. The pilgrimage was celebrated within a special edition of the popular journal *Current Archaeology* (volume 240), avidly read by more than 17,000 subscribers. The pilgrimage handbook, edited by Nick Hodgson, provides a very useful overview of research along the Wall over the previous decade. Also in 2009, a Research Framework for Hadrian's Wall, incorporating contributions from numerous experts, was published. This, it is hoped, will provide a sound basis for future research.

In March 2010, in an event to mark British Tourism Week and commemorate the 1600th anniversary of the end of Roman rule in Britain, hundreds of volunteers lit a line of beacons 500 metres apart along the full length of the Wall, from Wallsend to Bowness on Solway. This spectacular event enjoyed extensive press coverage and raised levels of interest in the Wall throughout Britain. Regardless of occasional such events, visitors continue to throng to the Wall at an estimated rate of half a million each year. Many visit the main forts, museums and other attractions along the Wall, while others are drawn by the challenge of walking all or part of the Hadrian's Wall Path National Trail, itself increasingly in demand for charity walks and other events. While all visitors are welcome, the task of enabling them to enjoy the landscape, while ensuring damage to the archaeological resource is minimised, now keeps a new army busy here – a small and constantly overworked army of heritage managers who are, it has to be said, rather poorly resourced relative to their Roman predecessors. Clearly, as we move towards the Wall's 1900th anniversary, it continues to enthral academics and general visitors alike, as it will probably continue to do for another 1900 years, and beyond.

In the very month (February 2013) that the final proof of this book was at last approved for publication, Erik P Graafstal published a fascinating academic paper entitled *Hadrian's haste: a priority programme for the Wall* (see references). This examines much of the material considered in this book relating to the chronology and sequence of construction of the Wall, but with more academic vigour than has been possible here. With some relief, I noted that Graafstal's general conclusions are remarkably similar to my own, though he also makes some further interesting observations relating in particular to the initial phases of construction; for example, he suggests that work on the Willowford section, including the bridge over the Irthing, may have been prioritised in order to facilitate its inspection by Hadrian in 122. Unfortunately, although a couple of brief references to it were hastily added to the text, there was no time to incorporate detailed discussion of this important paper, itself now essential reading for anyone interested in the subject.

Today, the Wall is regarded by most people as a magnificent military monument reflecting the glory of the Roman Empire. However, this public perception is based largely on interpretations by classical scholars extending back over three centuries. In fact, a perfectly reasonable case can be made, through the reinterpretation of the very same evidence, for the Wall to be considered largely as a monument to failure. In reality, the arguments are complex, and will keep academics busy for centuries to come, but it is my firm belief that alternative interpretations for this most famous of ancient monuments should be provided, in an accessible form, for the benefit of the general public.

This book presents a summary of what we know for sure about Hadrian and his Wall, along with some informed speculation. Some of the background material about Hadrian may not appear initially relevant to the Wall, but it is all fascinating and very relevant to our attempts to understand Hadrian's character, and thus to the mind that I believe dreamed up the concept of the Wall and personally dictated the initial blueprint. Whatever my own views, however, I must point out that on the basis of the available evidence it remains possible that Hadrian's direct involvement in the planning of the Wall was minimal, and that he simply ordered his officials to reinforce the frontier in whatever way they thought appropriate, as other emperors before and after him would have done.

Before concluding this brief introduction, I must acknowledge a huge debt of gratitude to all who have preceded me in the study of Hadrian's Wall, the most celebrated of whom are briefly mentioned towards the end of Chapter 2. Back in 1985, Brian Dobson (himself a giant amongst Wall scholars, who sadly left us in 2012) ended an influential paper entitled *The Function of Hadrian's Wall* with the words quoted at the head of this introduction. There have, indeed, been many giants in the field of Wall studies over the past three centuries, to whom we should all be truly grateful, but they are all dwarfed by the true giant ultimately responsible for this entire field of study: Hadrian himself, an extraordinary man, who, despite apparently widespread unpopularity at the time of his death, left a wonderful legacy that we are still able to enjoy in our twenty-first century world.

Since accepting the invitation to write this book, and forming my own general opinions as to Hadrian's probable personal involvement in the Wall project, I have noted that some, but by no means all, writers on the subject have suggested a similar scenario. All, however, are united in acknowledging that the evidence is ambiguous and will probably always remain so. That is precisely what makes it so interesting! Back in the mid-nineteenth century, at the very start of *The Roman Wall* (a magnificent book, now a bible for Wall scholars) John Collingwood Bruce observes that:

'A dead Wall may seem to many persons a very unpromising subject. The stones are indeed inanimate, but he who has a head to think, and a heart to feel, will find them suggestive of bright ideas and melting sympathies; though dead themselves, they will be the cause of mental life in him'.

In the spirit of these words, I invite you, the reader, to consider what follows with an open mind. I encourage you to form your own opinions as to why the Wall was built, how it functioned, the extent to which Hadrian was personally involved in the project, and whether, in the final analysis, it should be regarded as a magnificent success that achieved its objectives (whatever they may have been), a ridiculously over-elaborate white elephant that was always doomed to ultimate failure, or perhaps a bit of both.

Chapter 1

Hadrian

Few great men have been so much admired, so seldom comprehended and so little loved.

Royston Lambert, 1984.

Austere and genial, affable and harsh, hesitant and impetuous, mean and generous, deceitful and straightforward, cruel and merciful, and always, in all things, changeable.

Historia Augusta (late 4th century AD).

Introduction

In order to approach an understanding of Hadrian's Wall, it is necessary to attempt an understanding of the man ultimately responsible for its construction. This, however, is not easy; Hadrian was hugely enigmatic in his lifetime and remains so today. A legitimate case can be made for regarding him as one of the most brilliant leaders in the history of mankind, who, despite a tragic personal life, always sought to rule as 'first among equals' rather than as a dictator. Alternatively, the historical and archaeological evidence can be interpreted to present him as an ambitious, arrogant, devious and vain megalomaniac who became emperor by default and whose main objective throughout his reign was self-glorification. His supporters stress the generally peaceful nature of his reign, his shunning of warfare as a route to glory, and his stabilisation of the empire's borders. His detractors argue that his policy of non-expansion was the beginning of the end for the empire, the effective maintenance of which demanded a regular diet of military conquests. Either way (and the truth must lie somewhere between these two extremes) Hadrian continues to command respect as one of the most famous figures from antiquity, having ruled the vast Roman Empire, extending from the Scottish Borders to the Sahara and from the Atlantic to Arabia, for 21 years between 117 and his death in 138.

Hadrian wrote an autobiography towards the end of his life but, although a little of it survives incorporated within later works, it is almost entirely lost. There are two main literary sources that provide information about his life. The first of these is the *History of Rome* compiled by Cassius Dio, a senator from north-west Turkey, in the early third century. Within this vast eighty-volume work, volume 69 coverered Hadrian's reign; much of it is now lost but, fortunately, substantial extracts survive incorporated within later works. The second source is the anonymous 'Life of Hadrian' contained within the *Historia Augusta*, a key work containing biographies of several Roman emperors compiled from earlier sources, probably in the 390s. This contains much unsubstantiated speculation (some of which is clearly inaccurate) but remains, nevertheless, a crucial source. Along with occasional references by other classical writers, these sources combine with information gleaned from inscriptions, monuments and coins from throughout the empire to allow us to create the following quite detailed, though admittedly patchy and occasionally somewhat speculative, biography. (Note that in the interests of continuity and readability this account does not provide original references for all episodes; readers wishing to consult original sources should consult the references at the end of the book). Over recent centuries Hadrian has generally enjoyed a positive press, but readers are invited to interpret the following account for themselves and thus form their own views of Rome's enigmatic fourteenth emperor.

A privileged childhood, AD 76-94

Publius Aelius Hadrianus was born, probably in Rome, on 24th January 76. His parents were both Spanish but his father, Publius Aelius Hadrianus Afer, was a senator (the Senate consisted of the top 600 Roman aristocrats) so the family resided primarily in Rome. His father's family was based at Italica (a small Roman town originally founded in the late third century BC for wounded veterans) near Seville. His mother, Domitia Paulina, came from Cadiz, a very wealthy Roman city. He had one sibling, an elder sister, also called Domitia Paulina, of whom he was apparently not at all fond. The family's great wealth was based largely on ownership of extensive and very productive olive groves; vast quantities of olive oil were exported from this region of Spain to Rome and throughout the empire. Publius was Hadrian's first name (the Roman equivalent of a Christian name), Aelius was his father's family name, and Hadrianus refers to the port of Hadria (after which the Adriatic Sea is named) from which his father's family traced its origins prior to the move to Italica. Hadrian was looked after from birth by a German slave wet-nurse, Germana, who outlived him and with whom he maintained a close friendship throughout his life. Some commentators have cited the infant

Hadrian's essentially 'loveless' family as a defining influence on his character, underlining many aspects of his adult life which, as we will see, seems to have been essentially loveless, even lonely, for much of the time.

Although born into a wealthy and influential family, Hadrian was not related in any way to the emperor, Vespasian, and throughout his childhood no one could have guessed that he would one day become emperor. Given his family background, he could reasonably aspire to follow in his father's footsteps as a senator, but when he was just nine years old we encounter what, in retrospect, can be regarded as the single most significant event in his life. His father died and he was placed under the joint guardianship of his father's cousin, Marcus Ulpius Traianus (who would later become one of Rome's most celebrated emperors, known to history as Trajan), and a prominent man from Italica, Publius Acilius Attianus. Little is known of his childhood, which was spent in Rome, although he was apparently a very intelligent child and keen from an early age on all things Greek, so much so that he earned the nickname *'Graeculus'* ('the little Greek'). This obsessive fascination with Greek culture would have a profound impact on his later life.

When he was 14, he travelled to the ancestral home at Italica and underwent some military training within the *iuvenes*, a kind of 'aristocratic cadet force' founded by Augustus (Rome's first emperor and a constant inspiration and role model to Hadrian). This provided classes in patriotism and military matters for upper-class young men throughout the empire. He also spent much time and money hunting, which would become a lifelong passion. Trajan, himself fond of the hunt but apparently not to the same obsessive degree as Hadrian, considered his adolescent ward to be wasting time, and soon recalled him to Rome.

The ancient sources make it clear that Hadrian was intrigued by aspects of what we might refer to today as the occult, or astrology. This interest may have started early in life, as while in Italica he apparently consulted a great-uncle, an expert astrologer, who predicted the young Hadrian would one day become emperor. Such a prediction, had it become public, would have represented a death warrant during the tyrannical reign of Domitian (son of Vespasian) who reigned from 81-96. If the story is true then both parties must have kept it a secret; it is usually assumed that its source was Hadrian's lost autobiography, written at a time when the tale could no longer do any harm. Such a mind-blowing prediction may, of course, have involved a degree of wishful thinking on the part of the great-uncle, but it is nevertheless intriguing to speculate that, from this point on, Hadrian may genuinely have believed he was destined to become emperor.

Political and military life, AD 94-117

In the year 94, aged 18, Hadrian took up his first public position. He became a member of the 'Board of Ten', a one-year appointment presiding over various civil suits within the law courts. This was followed by a ceremonial appointment with the equestrians (the second tier of the Roman aristocracy, below the senators), and, in spring 95, by a spell as deputy to the Consuls. The Consuls, of which there were normally two each year, were the chief Roman magistrates. Although the role was largely symbolic, a consulship was considered very prestigious and was generally regarded as the pinnacle of a senatorial career; many emperors appointed themselves to the role. Each spring, by long established tradition, the two incumbent Consuls travelled to a sanctuary of Jupiter outside Rome and had to appoint a temporary deputy to cover for them while they were away. It was to this position that Hadrian was briefly appointed.

Trajan, by now a trusted general of the increasingly paranoid emperor, Domitian, was instrumental in planning the young Hadrian's early career. It was soon time for some real military experience; his first appointment was as tribune (nominally second-in-command) of *Legion II Adiutrix*, stationed at the time at Aquincum (Budapest) on the Danubian frontier within the province of Pannonia. A few years previously, this legion had played a major role in Agricola's successful campaigns in northern Britain. Hadrian will doubtless have discussed much about Britain with the men of his legion, many of whom will have had stories to tell of the wild northern frontier. After about a year, Hadrian left this legion and took up a second tribunate, this time with the *Legion V Macedonica* stationed at Oescus (Gigen) in Lower Moesia, also on the Danube. It was unusual for anyone to take a second commission like this, though Trajan had done so some years previously; we may assume that Hadrian was enjoying the military life and that Trajan's influence was instrumental in securing him both positions. We don't know how much active service he saw during his two tribunates, but both legions were involved in campaigns against the powerful Dacians.

For the benefit of readers unfamiliar with the subject, we must briefly divert from the life of Hadrian to say something about the basic structure of the army he served in, and would later command. The Roman army was fundamental to the management of the empire and a brief understanding of it is essential to what follows throughout the rest of this book. The army had several branches, of which the security of the empire rested largely with three: the legions, the auxiliaries and the fleet. The legions, of which there were 28, each consisted of a little more than 5,000 well-trained, well-equipped infantry together with a small detachment of 120 cavalry; thus the total legionary force (if all units were at full strength, which was rarely if ever the case) was about 150,000 men. The legions only recruited Roman citizens, though it seems that many recruits had no genuine claim to citizenship and were granted it unofficially upon enlistment. Each legion contained a wide range of skilled men such as architects, surveyors, masons, carpenters, blacksmiths, engineers, mechanics, and medics. The auxiliary units (from the Latin 'auxilia' – literally 'helpers') were mostly infantry, cavalry or mixed units, consisting of either 500 or 1,000 men. In addition there were also specialist units, such as archers, slingers and scouts. Most auxiliary soldiers were not Roman citizens, but were granted Roman citizenship upon retirement thus bringing them various social privileges and earning their sons the right to serve in a legion. It is impossible to know the exact numbers, but in Hadrian's time about 60% of soldiers were auxiliaries; a total of some 220,000 men (150,000 infantry and 70,000 cavalry) spread throughout nearly 400 auxiliary units. Along with three legions, more than fifty auxiliary units (some 36,000 men) were based in Britain – more than in any other province. The vast majority of both legions and auxiliary units were based in frontier provinces, in many of which they were assisted by the fleet, or navy, which played a crucial role in the management and defence of frontiers, as well as fighting piracy and supplying distant garrisons. The navy seems to have been generally regarded as somewhat less prestigious than the auxiliary units, but men received Roman citizenship on retirement in the same way. There were many provincial fleets based around the fringes of the empire, for example the British fleet and those on the Rhine, the Danube, and the Black Sea, in addition to those that patrolled parts of the Mediterranean. In the absence of any kind of police force or customs control, all such duties were performed by soldiers, as were numerous other tasks including military and civilian building projects and the management of industrial activity within mining zones.

Turning our attention back to Hadrian, at this stage in his life few people could have seriously entertained the idea of him ever becoming emperor, but events wholly outside his control were now to catapult him into a position from which the top job must have appeared genuinely attainable. These events began with the assassination of Domitian, in September 96. Domitian was succeeded by Marcus Cocceius Nerva, an elderly senator who did not enjoy the support of the army and who seems to have been generally regarded as stop-gap appointment. Nerva had no natural heir, and announced that he had adopted Trajan, by now a very popular military commander, to be his successor. Nerva cited divine guidance when making this decision, but, given his unpopularity within the army, he probably had no choice if he wished to avoid a military coup. The man who had been Hadrian's guardian, effectively his adoptive father, thus became heir to the imperial throne.

Hadrian, extraordinarily, now took up a third tribunate, this time with the *Legion XXII Primigenia*, stationed at Mogontiacum (Mainz) in Upper Germany where his brother-in-law, Julius Servianus, was governor. Trajan was stationed at Cologne, to the north in Lower Germany. When Nerva died in Rome in January 98, Trajan was immediately declared emperor. The instant this news reached Upper Germany, Hadrian set off northwards with the intention of delivering the news in person to his adoptive father. Servianus (himself a contender to become Trajan's heir) sent a messenger of his own to deliver the news northwards, having allegedly tried to sabotage Hadrian's attempt to get there first. Hadrian, however, won the race, and thus had the honour of informing the new emperor of his accession. Trajan went on to become a hugely popular warrior-emperor, ruling with the unwavering support of the army for two decades during which he became known as *Optimus Princeps* ('the Best of Princes'). Ever the warrior, Trajan continued to serve on the Rhine-Danube frontier for nearly two years after his accession, returning to Rome as emperor towards the end of 99.

Hadrian enjoyed a very close relationship with Trajan's wife, Pompeia Plotina, perhaps based to an extent on their shared love of all things Greek. Plotina seems to have played a role in organising Hadrian's marriage to Trajan's grand-niece, Vibia Sabina. The marriage probably took place sometime in the year 100, when Sabina was 14 (a normal age for girls to be married at the time) and Hadrian 24. Little is known about Sabina, although we do know that she had her own mansion in Rome and a large personal household, with an independent income from brickyards and other interests. The nature of the marriage was somewhat peculiar from the start. Just as Trajan was married to Plotina yet sought sexual gratification with young boys, so Hadrian was married to Sabina and also preferred sex with boys. One ancient reference records that Hadrian also had adulterous liaisons with married women, and thus that he may have been bisexual, but there is no supporting evidence for this; indeed, his own marriage may never have been consummated. Hadrian, it seems, was homosexual, but there was nothing particularly unusual about this in ancient Rome. His marriage was not based on mutual love and affection, but was an economic and political arrangement of convenience to both parties. Regardless of the nature of the marriage, Hadrian was now effectively related to the childless Trajan on two counts. He, and others, must surely have realised by this stage that he had a decent chance of eventually succeeding his emperor.

In 101, Trajan began his first war against the Dacians beyond the Danube. Hadrian, back in Rome, became 'Quaestor of the Emperor', a distinguished position that involved reading all the emperor's speeches and letters to the senate. We are told that he had something of a rustic accent that the senators found amusing: exactly why this should have been the case is not clear, but he practiced his public speaking and soon put things right.

At some point, Hadrian joined Trajan on campaign in Dacia. Trajan was a heavy drinker, something else, in addition to a penchant for young boys, that he and Hadrian apparently had in common. We can imagine the two of them enjoying drinking sessions with senior officers at the battle-front; perhaps the bond between the two men became stronger during such sessions.

In 102, again back in Rome, Hadrian took up a new appointment as 'Tribune of the Plebs', a once powerful but now largely symbolic position representing the people on the Senate. Subsequently, in 105, he became a *Praetor*, a kind of magistrate; his particular duties included the popular business of arranging games and festivals for the people. These positions gave him practical experience in government, including first-hand experience of the workings of the Senate, that would be of much value to him in later times.

Hadrian returned to military duty in 106 when war broke out again in Dacia. He was made commander of *Legion I Minervia*, based in Bonn but moved to the Danube during the earlier Dacian conflict. He was decorated for his role in the fighting, as he had been during the earlier campaign. When this war was over, Trajan opted to annex Dacia and transform it into a fully-fledged Roman province; after the previous campaign it had been left as a nominally independent kingdom though under heavy Roman influence. Hadrian was now appointed as governor of the province of Lower Pannonia and commander of the province's only legion, *II Adiutrix* (the first legion in which he had served, a decade previously), based at Budapest. In this role he was praised for his efficient management of both military and civilian matters, gaining particular praise for his military discipline.

In May 108, Hadrian was appointed to the ancient and prestigious position of Consul, the most senior position available to a senator. Most men who achieved this position did so in their forties, but Hadrian had made it by the relatively young age of 32. On top of this he had served as tribune with three different legions, had fought in two wars, had commanded a legion and governed a province. Few people in the empire now had a more impressive cv than Hadrian, who was of course also related to the childless Trajan, both through his adoption and his marriage.

We cannot be sure whether Trajan ever discussed the issue of his successor with Hadrian, but the two continued to enjoy a close relationship. Hadrian worked for a while as imperial speechwriter, and involved himself to some extent in Trajan's spectacular building projects in Rome. He fancied himself as an architect, although his views apparently found little favour with Trajan's chief architect, Apollodorus, who thought little of his advice and advised him to steer clear of practical building projects. In the fullness of time, as we will see shortly, Hadrian's building projects would become rather better known than those of Apollodorus.

It was probably in 111 or 112 that Hadrian visited Greece for the first time. We have already noted that he was very fond of all things Greek from an early age, and his first visit to Athens must have been a hugely exciting time for him. In 112 he accepted the ancient office of 'archon', chief magistrate of the city, and the Athenians erected a statue of him in the Theatre of Dionysus, below the Acropolis. The base of this statue incorporates an inscription detailing Hadrian's career to date; the positions are set out in reverse order, beginning with the consulship in 108 and ending with his first public position with the 'Board of Ten' back in 94:

To Publius Aelius Hadrianus, son of Publius, Sergian voting-division, consul, member of the Board of Seven for Ritual Banquets, member of the Brotherhood of the Cult of Augustus, governor in Lower Pannonia of the emperor Nerva Trajan Caesar Augustus conqueror of Germany, conqueror of Dacia, praetor and at the same time commander of the First Legion, Minerva's dutiful and loyal, in the Dacian War, tribune of the plebs, quaestor of the emperor Trajan and his companion in the Dacian Expedition, decorated by the emperor twice, tribune of the Second Legion, the rescuers, dutiful and loyal, and of the Fifth, the Conquerors of Macedon, and of the Twenty-Second, First-born Fortune's, dutiful and loyal, leader of the squadron of Roman knights, in charge of the City of Rome during the Latin festival, judge of the Board of Ten.

This is very impressive career for one still so young; perhaps many in Athens already regarded Hadrian as Trajan's likely successor, half a decade before he would become emperor.

Trajan now embarked on another war, this time against the Parthians who occupied Mesopotamia and posed something of a threat to Rome's eastern frontier. The pretext for the war was the appointment by the Parthians of a new King of Armenia without reference to Rome; under the terms of an earlier treaty the Parthians were allowed to nominate Armenian monarchs but no king could be crowned without Rome's blessing. This, however, is unlikely to have been the sole reason for the conflict which surely owed its origin in large part to Trajan's expansionist policy in the east. Trajan travelled to the war zone via Athens, perhaps picking up Hadrian en route. From there he sailed to Syria, a province of vital strategic importance to the Parthian War, where Hadrian was appointed governor, based at Antioch. During 116, the Roman army occupied the Parthian capital, Ctesiphon, on the Tigris, and southern Mesopotamia was declared a new Roman province to be known as Assyria. The Roman Empire had reached its maximum size, extending from central Britain across Europe to Africa and eastwards across Dacia and Parthia to the Tigris, but many problems were brewing. Mesopotamia, only recently annexed, rose in rebellion, and there was a major revolt involving Jewish communities in Cyprus, Cyrenaica and Egypt. Had Trajan been a younger man, he may well have acted swiftly to crush these uprisings, and may also have opted to expand the empire still further eastwards in the footsteps of Alexander the Great, but he was now in his sixties and his health began to falter. He decided to return to Rome but didn't make it, dying at Selinus in Cicilia (southern Turkey) in August 117.

Becoming emperor, AD 117-121

According to the *Historia Augusta*, it was widely believed that Trajan intended to die without having adopted an heir, leaving instead a shortlist from which the Senate should choose his successor. It was on his deathbed that he is said to have announced his decision to adopt Hadrian, a decision always regarded as suspicious, with many commentators questioning whether it was actually made by the dying emperor or by his wife, Plotina, who, as we have already seen, was a close friend of Hadrian. Few others were present with Trajan at the time he supposedly announced this momentous decision; in addition to Plotina, those present included Matidia (Trajan's niece and Hadrian's mother in law) and Publius Acilius Attianus, by this time Trajan's personal bodyguard, who had acted as Hadrian's co-guardian (alongside Trajan) following the death of his father three decades earlier. We will never know to what extent Trajan was responsible for the decision, but one thing we can be certain of is that Plotina, Matidia and Attianus would all have been happy to see Hadrian take over.

Intrigue over the succession is lent further weight by the mysterious case of Marcus Ulpius Phaedimus, Trajan's personal butler who we may assume remained loyal to his master until the end. Phaedimus' gravestone records that he died at Selinus on 12th August 117, precisely the day on which the world was informed of Trajan's death and Hadrian's accession, and that his remains were relocated to Rome (presumably having previously been buried locally) a dozen years later. Why should Phaedimus have died at the same time as Trajan? Did he know too much? Was he quietly removed from the scene and buried in Selinus until any potential fuss over the accession had died down? We will never know the answers to these questions, but they certainly add weight to the rumours about the legitimacy of Hadrian's accession. We may also note in passing that Plotina and Matidia, loyal members of Trajan's female-dominated imperial household, were retained by Hadrian as key members of his own imperial family, while Attianus would soon be honourably retired to a prestigious position of relatively little influence.

Whatever occurred at Selinus, Hadrian, still stationed at Antioch, assumed full power immediately upon the announcement of Trajan's death. At the age of 41, he had become the most powerful man in the world, but his position was initially far from secure. He quickly, and very wisely, arranged a generous financial bonus for serving soldiers; he was promptly proclaimed *'imperator'* ('conqueror'), a prestigious title bestowed by the military, and throughout his reign he would enjoy the loyal support of the army. He was, however, destined never to be so popular with the Senate, as his reign began with a scandal from which he never fully recovered. Four prominent and much respected senators were executed within a few months of his accession, amid unsubstantiated rumours that they were plotting a coup. Hadrian always claimed that he had nothing to do with the matter, and that the executions were ordered and carried out without his authority. However, many thought him directly responsible, and his relations with the Senate were always strained as a result. That said, the Senate accepted his accession and approved his request for the deification of Trajan. The Senate also offered Hadrian the hugely honourable title of *Pater Patriae* (Father of the People), but the new emperor refused to accept it so early in his reign, following Augustus in stating that it should be earned through achievement rather than simply granted as a matter of course.

Hadrian's attitude towards imperial expansion was in marked contrast to that of Trajan. He sought consolidation rather than expansion, almost immediately giving up the three recently conquered Parthian provinces of Armenia, Assyria and Mesopotamia. He also gave up some of the land recently conquered from the Dacians, ordering the dismantling of Trajan's great bridge over the Danube so that the river again became the frontier at this point. Although this policy of consolidation is usually cited by commentators as commendable, we must ask to what extent Hadrian really had any choice. Trajan's expansionism had created many enemies at the fringes of the empire, and, as already noted, the army was increasingly overstretched. As Trajan had pushed south-eastwards towards the Persian Gulf, rebellions broke out in the 'conquered' lands behind. In Cyrenaica, Egypt and Cyprus a major Jewish uprising in 116, during which many thousands of civilians were killed, had necessitated large-scale military intervention to restore order. During the early years of Hadrian's reign 'the Britons could not be kept under Roman control', a statement usually interpreted as evidence of conflict on the northern frontier, though the scale of military activity is not recorded.

Hadrian, given his political and military experience and his knowledge of Roman history, surely realised that he had no option other than to give up Trajan's recently conquered lands, shun any thoughts of further expansion, and concentrate on the maintenance of order within the existing bounds of the empire.

This approach was unpopular with many, given the perceived glory associated with empire's triumphal expansion from its humble beginnings over previous centuries. Indeed, despite the advice of the first emperor, Augustus, to retain the empire within the boundaries he had established, many still thought it Rome's natural destiny to conquer and rule the entire world. Hadrian, however, was adamant; in direct opposition to the more hawkish elements within the Senate and the army, coins struck early in his reign bore slogans such as 'peace', 'justice', and 'piety'.

These coins, together with powerful statues erected in towns and cities throughout the empire, ensured that Hadrian's image soon became universally familiar. It was an unusual image for a Roman emperor. Earlier emperors were clean-shaven, but Hadrian had a full beard in the manner of a Greek philosopher. Some thought the beard was to hide a facial blemish, and beards were by no means unusual amongst Roman soldiers on active service, but most commentators see the imperial beard as another sign of its owner's love of all things Greek. It set a trend that would be followed by generations of emperors, and presumably many others in Roman society. By all accounts the new emperor cut an imposing figure, being tall and robustly built. In keeping with his robust figure, he had a healthy appetite; his favourite dish was said to be a kind of game pie consisting of meat from a variety of animals, no doubt reflecting his love of the hunt. He had a powerful face with strong nose, puckered brow and close-set, piercing, grey-blue eyes that have been described as 'weaselish'. The beard was kept neatly trimmed, and the imperial hair was regularly curled with tongs. His general countenance has been described as strained and joyless, but his firm expression on coins and statues is appropriate for a statesman and commander-in-chief.

Attempts to summarise Hadrian's character from the available sources are fraught with difficulty and seem always to feature words like 'complex', 'enigmatic' and 'elusive'. (Note here the quotations at the head of this chapter; we will have more to say about his character towards the end of the chapter). Clearly, he paid much attention to his physical appearance and it has been suggested that he was rather vain and insecure, perhaps even having something of an inferiority complex despite being the most powerful man in the Roman world. His insecurity is perhaps reflected in his alleged use of what we would today term 'secret police' to spy on colleagues and friends; though in the circumstances such activity is perhaps best regarded as plain common sense. He is said to have had considerable intellect and a prodigious memory, being able to undertake several tasks simultaneously and having a reputation for never forgetting peoples' names. He was greatly interested in the arts, notably architecture, poetry, sculpture and music (he was a keen flautist). He was also proficient at maths, having an in depth understanding of economics and taxation. He seems also to have had a genuine social conscience, stating that the law should combine justice with human kindness and championing legislation in favour of the humble. He believed that the empire belonged to the people and saw himself as a servant of the people, ruling as their representative rather than as a dictator as certain of his predecessors had done.

Like Trajan before him, Hadrian was in no great rush to return to Rome following his accession, remaining on duty on the eastern frontier for nearly a year. Eventually, in July 118, he returned to Rome as emperor, remaining here for the next three years while consolidating his hold on power. He organised very popular festivities for the people of Rome, for example in honour of Trajan and to celebrate his birthday in January 119, and further enhanced his general popularity by cancelling all taxation arrears throughout Rome and the provinces. He appointed himself Consul in 118 (this had already been promised to him by Trajan) and again in 119, and contributed positively to many Senate meetings and other official functions, taking personal interest in detailed matters that other emperors would have considered beneath them.

Architecture throughout the empire

Hadrian modelled himself in many ways on Augustus, notably in his desire to add architectural masterpieces to Rome and other cities of the empire. Once established as emperor, his passion for architecture knew no bounds. In addition to military projects (of which more later), he commissioned fabulous new buildings throughout the empire and, although clear evidence is lacking, does seem to have been closely involved in the initial design stages of many architectural projects. Previous emperors, not least Trajan, had been responsible for numerous magnificent buildings, but Hadrian with his abiding personal passion for architecture and his desire to avoid unnecessary military conflict, perhaps regarded his building projects as his main route to imperial glory. Here, and in the next two sections, we diverge from the generally chronological framework of this chapter to consider particular aspects of Hadrian's passion for architecture.

Hadrian was well aware of the potential power of architecture, both within the empire and amongst her enemies, and he exploited this with great expertise and enthusiasm. He must have employed several architects, and may have had one or more particular favourites, but details of them are lost; his buildings therefore tend to be ascribed simply to him. The *Historia Augusta* records that he 'built something in almost every city', and Hadrianic construction projects are indeed attested in more than fifty cities throughout the empire. These include temples, theatres, baths, stadia, granaries, aqueducts, roads, bridges, ports, city walls and gates, new residential districts, and even entire new cities; Hadrian founded, or re-founded, at least eight new cities that bear his name, while many other settlements officially changed their name to incorporate direct reference to their emperor in grateful acknowledgement of some act of imperial generosity. It is important to note that Hadrian's passion for architecture was not all about producing new things for people to marvel at in the future; his fascination with the past is also demonstrated architecturally through the conservation of numerous ancient temples, tombs, shrines and other structures deemed by him to be of historical importance. In this he was clearly concerned with the preservation and promotion of the unique histories of specific places (what we might today term the celebration of local distinctiveness) and through such work helped to forge perceived links between himself and many great characters and events of the distant past.

Of particular importance are projects within Rome and at Tivoli in Italy (covered in the following two sections) and in Athens (discussed later), but many further projects will be also be noted in the context of Hadrian's travels throughout his empire in the remainder of this chapter. These projects were about much more than simply the provision of magnificent buildings; while the buildings did indeed provide a splendid backdrop for everyday life, they also played a crucial role in creating and cementing political relationships between emperor, local elites and the people, while also providing meaningful employment for countless thousands of architects, engineers, craftsmen and builders at often vast building sites spread throughout the empire. The provision of new buildings should not be considered in isolation as they were often linked to the prestigious enhancement of a city's status, or the granting or embellishment of festivals, including games. We know that Hadrian was personally responsible for the establishment, or reinvigoration, of festivals (including games) at more than twenty cities; these were not simply for the short-term pleasure of the people but were of lasting economic importance to the cities concerned as they attracted large numbers of visitors from far and wide.

Dio's *History of Rome* relates an unsavoury incident that often underpins views of Hadrian as an architect. It is recorded that Hadrian ordered the execution of Trajan's chief architect, Apollodorus of Damascus, following the latter's criticism of plans for the new Temple of Venus and Roma (discussed below). Hadrian had apparently sent him the plans to demonstrate that magnificent buildings could be designed and built by others, but Apollodorus replied by pointing out several perceived faults in the design. Such insolence was sufficient, according to Dio, to warrant the architect's execution. The story also notes that Hadrian's antipathy towards Apollodorus extended back much earlier to a meeting with Trajan; during discussion of some architectural matter Apollodorus had told Hadrian to 'be off and draw your pumpkins. You do not understand any of these matters'. According to the story, Hadrian's simmering resentment of this incident led eventually to his order to execute Apollodorus, the disagreement over the Temple of Venus and Roma providing no more than a convenient excuse.

Many present-day scholars doubt that Hadrian would actually have ordered the execution of Apollodorus, but whether he did or not, the story serves to demonstrate Hadrian's great interest in architecture, involving himself directly in the detailed planning of new buildings. It has been suggested that the 'pumpkins' that Hadrian was apparently drawing may have been experimental designs for domes employing new concrete technology, demonstrating a close interest in contemporary architectural developments long before he became emperor.

Rebuilding Rome

Augustus is said to have stated that he 'found Rome brick, and left it marble'. While there is no evidence to suggest that Augustus was personally involved in architectural design, he certainly had a dramatic effect on the appearance of the city, one on which Hadrian was keen to build, reflecting his personal passion for architecture. He commissioned and restored numerous magnificent buildings that collectively provided the stage on which the ceremonial and everyday life of the city was enacted. The Hadrianic 'building boom' within Rome provided employment for thousands of skilled and unskilled workers including architects, engineers, builders, stonemasons, brick and tile manufacturers, carpenters and hauliers, all working together to enhance the glory of their emperor and their city. Individual citizens, whether directly involved in construction work or not, must have felt huge pride as their city was transformed with splendid new buildings and much-loved historic buildings were restored and enhanced. Although ancient architectural traditions of Greece and Rome were much respected, Hadrian and his architects also combined exotic materials from distant sources with new ways of using brick and concrete to develop radical new designs for some projects. When in the city, Hadrian resided in Domitian's opulent palace on the Palatine Hill, though he seems not to have sought to embellish this, preferring instead to concentrate his efforts on communal buildings within the city and his great villa at Tivoli. Amongst the many Hadrianic buildings in Rome, three demand specific attention here: the Pantheon, the Temple of Venus and Roma, and Hadrian's mausoleum with the adjacent *Pons Aelius*.

The Pantheon

Work was underway on arguably Hadrian's single most extraordinary building very soon after his accession. The building in question is the Pantheon, a truly magnificent structure still regarded with awe by visitors to Rome today. Hadrian's version of the Pantheon replaced an earlier building that was destroyed by fire after being struck by lightning in 110, this having itself replaced the original structure built by Marcus Vipsanius Agrippa (son-in-law of Augustus) in about 25 BC and destroyed by fire in AD 80. Little is known of these earlier structures, although limited archaeological investigations suggest they had similar plans and alignments to the surviving building.

Hadrian's Pantheon survives today as undeniably one of the world's most important and famous ancient buildings; it really does have to be experienced at first hand to be fully appreciated. Described by Michelangelo in the early sixteenth century, as 'of angelic not human design', it has enthralled visitors and fascinated students of architecture for nearly two millennia. It was reconsecrated as a Christian church in 609, since when it has been continually maintained and consequently survives remarkably intact into the modern era.

The Pantheon is entered through an impressive but outwardly relatively conventional front porch, consisting of a massive gable supported on twelve-metre high columns surmounted with intricately carved capitals of white marble. Close inspection, however, reveals the columns to be anything but conventional; they are of distinctive grey and pink Egyptian granite, quarried from the desert and transported to Rome in what must have been a complex logistical operation. Quarrying the columns must in itself have posed huge problems, but once quarried each column, weighing 80 tons, had to be carted 100km across the desert to the Nile, loaded onto barges and floated downriver to the Mediterranean coast, then transferred to ocean-going vessels for the journey to Rome. Even after this, getting them from the harbour to the site of the Pantheon was no simple task. Despite all these logistical challenges, however, they were duly procured and erected as required.

After passing through the great entrance porch, through its forest of columns and beneath its original grand ceiling of bronze, the visitor reached two huge bronze doors, beyond which is the vast, breathtaking space of the main rotunda. The architecture of this rotunda is astonishing. Its colossal domed roof, the largest unreinforced concrete dome anywhere in the world, measures 43 metres in diameter and weighs an estimated 5,000 tons. It sits above a cylinder of precisely the same height, so that if the curve of the roof is extended to the floor it forms a perfect sphere. It is still not known exactly how the roof was constructed, but the process must have involved the use of temporary wooden supports on a huge scale. Originally decorated, probably in bronze, the dome's five rings of twenty-eight coffers are now plain, drawing the eye up to the central occulus, nine metres in diameter, through which the entire rotunda is dramatically illuminated by natural sunlight.

While attention is understandably focussed on this magnificent roof, the floor and walls of the rotunda are also extraordinary, being beautifully decorated with columns and geometric patterns of marble and other precious stone obtained from many different sources throughout the empire. Seven large niches, interspersed with raised shrines, are arranged geometrically around the walls of the rotunda; these would originally have contained grand statues of gods and emperors.

The original purpose of the Pantheon is unknown, though its name suggests it functioned as a temple to all the gods. We know that statues of several gods and members of the imperial family stood within it, and its location suggests it may have been symbolically linked in some way to the Mausoleum of Augustus which shares the same architectural axis at a distance of some 750 metres. The occulus suggests a link with the heavens; the sun would have shone through it at different angles, highlighting particular sectors of the interior at different times of day, varying according to the seasons. We know Hadrian held court within the Pantheon, suggesting he regarded it as of supreme importance within the complex symbolic architecture of the city.

A further observation to make with regard to the Pantheon is that its design may well been drawn up under Trajan by his chief architect – who was, of course, Apollodorus. The dating of the monument does not allow us to be sure whether it was Trajan or Hadrian who instituted the project, but how ironic it would be if the great dome of the Pantheon was somehow linked to Hadrian's 'pumpkins', and in fact owed more to Apollodorus than to Hadrian, to whom it is now credited. Without doubt, however, it was Hadrian who saw the structure completed, and to complicate matters further he had a copy of the dedication inscription from the original Pantheon (stating 'Marcus Agrippa......made this') prominently displayed above the façade of the new structure. This fooled antiquarians over several centuries into thinking that this part of the monument survived from the original structure, but recent studies of dated bricks now demonstrate that the entire structure is Hadrianic. Exactly why Hadrian should have done this, when he could easily have placed his own name here instead, is not known; perhaps it was a genuine desire to see the original architect duly credited, just possibly linked to a wish to ensure that Apollodorus, if indeed he had been involved in the project, was not to be celebrated as its architect. Elsewhere in Rome, Hadrian restored many other great buildings, including several temples, which he re-dedicated in the names of their original builders. The *Historia Augusta* records that he built public buildings 'in all places and without number', but only included his own name on one – the temple of his adoptive father, Trajan. This is in marked contrast to the discredited Domitian, who also oversaw an extraordinary building programme throughout Rome, including the restoration of many ancient buildings, but whose restoration projects (according to ancient sources) were all inscribed with his own name, with no mention of the original builders.

The detailed interpretation of the Pantheon's architecture presents many puzzles that cannot concern us here, though there can be no doubt that Hadrian regarded it as amongst his most significant building projects. Despite its scale, however, work was underway concurrently on a number of other buildings in the immediate vicinity using many of the same exotic materials, most notably the hugely impressive Temple of the Deified Trajan and the Temple of the Deified Matidia (Hadrian's mother-in-law who died in 119) which used columns even greater in size that those of the Pantheon. Evidently, even a project as grand as the Pantheon was insufficient in itself to satisfy Hadrian's obsession with grand architecture; from very early in his reign, he was clearly intent on leaving his mark on the capital on the grandest possible scale.

The Temple of Venus and Roma

The magnificent Temple of Venus and Roma brought classic Greek architecture, on a colossal scale, to the centre of Rome. It was intended as the spectacular focus for the new festival of the *Romaia*, a celebration of Rome's origins and achievements devised by Hadrian to replace the existing festival of the *Parilia*. (The twin dedication to Venus and Roma is explained by the former's role as patron deity of the imperial family, thus providing a direct link to Hadrian). To a large extent the cult of Roma within the Roman Empire was inspired by the ancient link between Athena and Athens; Hadrian saw it as a great unifying cult, attractive to Roman citizens throughout the empire, and the festival of *Romaia* was indeed celebrated enthusiastically on 21st April each year, nowhere more so than within the city of Rome itself. Hadrian used the term *Romae aeternae* when referring to the cult of Roma; to this day Rome remains universally known as the Eternal City.

The temple was the largest ever built in Rome and took a decade to complete between the mid 120s and mid 130s. It was built at the heart of the city, between the Forum and the Colosseum; in order to accommodate its vast platform (measuring 145 by 100 metres) in such a prestigious location, earlier buildings were demolished and a ten-metre high bronze statue of Helios (the sun god) was carefully dismantled to be re-erected elsewhere. The temple had two rows of twenty marble columns along each long side, with three rows of ten columns at each end; its form thus echoed the unfinished Temple of Zeus in Athens (about which we will have more to say shortly). The temple's interior consisted of two great chambers, square in plan, one of which contained a statue of Venus, the other a statue of Roma. The original Hadrianic temple was badly damaged by fire in the early fourth century, and today's fragmentary remains belong largely to a subsequent rebuild; it takes a great deal of imagination to envisage Hadrian's truly awe-inspiring original.

Hadrian's mausoleum and the Pons Aelius

Another monumental building that seems to have been under construction soon after Hadrian's accession is his vast mausoleum. In addition to be being another extraordinary architectural achievement, this was of immense symbolic significance. Nerva was the last emperor to be laid to rest within the great mausoleum of Augustus. Trajan's and Plotina's ashes were interred at the foot of Trajan's Column at the heart of the city. Hadrian decreed it was now time for a new imperial mausoleum to supercede that of Augustus. This was intended to house his own ashes and, in due course, those of his successors. Evidence from brick stamps suggests work was underway on the new mausoleum by about 123, but the project was so vast that it would not be completed within Hadrian's lifetime. The chosen site was on the west bank of the Tiber, linked to the city via a magnificent new bridge, the *Pons Aelius*. The location of the mausoleum on the west bank has drawn comparison with the Valley of the Kings in Egypt, where the west bank of the Nile was regarded as the home of the dead, but it is more likely that this was simply the most appropriate available location for a magnificent new structure designed to dominate its surroundings and to be very visible from the city. The basic structure was a huge drum, 70 metres in diameter and 30 metres high, atop a 15 metre high square base measuring 80 by 80 metres. A tower with its own vaulted chamber stood on top of the dome, and the whole magnificent edifice was probably crowned with a colossal statue of Hadrian, perhaps in a chariot being flown up to the heavens by eagles. The ten-metre high burial chamber, reached via a grand, curved corridor, was located within the main drum. The building's basic superstructure was of brick, concrete and travertine, on huge concrete foundations, but it was embellished with much ornate stonework, exotic marbles, mosaic floors and painted stucco ceilings. The interior was furnished with numerous great statues (of Hadrian amongst others), some on a colossal scale, while the exterior was embellished with bronze peacocks, horses and other figures. The monument functioned as the imperial mausoleum through until the early third century, and was transformed into a military fortress in 401. This was attacked and damaged by Goths during their fifth- and sixth-century invasions of Rome, and during medieval times it was redeveloped as the papal fortress, the Castel Sant'Angelo. Retaining its Hadrianic core, it remains a hugely impressive monument within today's city, still reached via the *Pons Aelius* which, despite much rebuilding over the centuries, still retains much of its original Hadrianic structure.

The Villa Adriana (Hadrian's villa) at Tivoli

No project demonstrates Hadrian's obsession with architecture more eloquently than his exquisite 'villa' at Tivoli, 28km east of Rome. Hadrian inherited a number of fine imperial villas, constructed by Trajan and others, but the chance to construct his own, on an unprecedented scale, was an opportunity he was not going to spurn. Described by Thorsten Opper as 'a vast architectural playground, with some structures that had no equal in the ancient world', it was more like a private city than a conventional villa. Its overall extent is not known for sure, but it is thought to extend over at least 120 hectares; if classified as a villa then it must surely be the most impressive villa in the world. It must have had a permanent staff of thousands ranging from senior officials down to an army of slaves, and there was presumably a permanent military presence to guarantee the emperor's security at all times. Much of the complex is yet to be explored by archaeologists, but already nearly a thousand rooms are known, including many unique structures built with extravagant materials and splendidly decorated, all linked together by a network of corridors and underground passageways.

Hadrian seems to have begun work on the villa soon after his accession. He may have owned the site before becoming emperor, but would not have had the resources to develop it as he did without access to the imperial coffers. Despite his frequent lengthy absences from Rome, construction work on the villa's multitude of buildings continued through until about 130. Hadrian used the complex as an alternative seat of government, effectively enabling him to 'work from home' whenever he chose, rather than travel into the city. Exactly why he chose this site for the villa is not known, though it is possible that his family already owned land here, and an existing villa on the site may have belonged to him or Sabina; whatever the explanation it was an inspired choice. The rural landscape setting is sublime, yet the site is far from isolated as a main road provided links to the nearby town of Tibur and to Rome; additionally, the nearby River Aniene was navigable, enabling architectural and other supplies to be brought in by boat.

As with all of Hadrian's architectural projects, the extent to which he may have been personally involved in planning and construction is open to question, but the villa does seem to have been built to an original grand master plan which necessitated the transformation of the natural landscape into a series of terraces, the setting out of particular zones for different functions (including palaces, the emperor's private quarters, guest rooms, and servants' quarters), the construction of complex fresh water and sewerage systems and a network of passageways (many of which were concealed below ground), and the laying out of exquisite gardens. Although Hadrian must have employed many architects on the project, it is surely beyond question that he must have been closely involved in the drawing up of the original plans; indeed, it is far from implausible that he dreamt up the original blueprint largely on his own, with a crack team of architects together with an army of specialist builders and craftsmen employed to transform his dream into reality. It appears that the plans were amended in several places while construction work was in progress, either to overcome unforeseen problems or to take advantage of new ideas. (This 'tinkering' with an original master plan is something we will encounter later on Hadrian's Wall, though evidence as to the extent to which the emperor was personally involved in initiating or approving such changes remains frustratingly elusive.)

Today, the vast ruins at Tivoli are hugely impressive and certainly evocative of Hadrian and his world, but they give only a hint of the villa's original grandeur as the buildings have been stripped of exotic materials and countless stunning statues and other beautiful works of art. An especially high status building on its own little island at the heart of the complex, known in modern times as the 'maritime theatre', was perhaps Hadrian's private retreat. Bricks dated to 117 demonstrate that this was one of the earliest structures completed, so Hadrian may have resided here while directing operations throughout the rest of the villa complex over subsequent years.

Other very high status buildings were presumably reserved for the emperor, his immediate family, the most senior officials and illustrious guests. These had walls and floors of expensive marble, some having multicoloured mosaics of the very highest quality. Lesser rooms had painted walls and many had exquisite black-and-white mosaic floors. Service rooms and servants' quarters were generally spacious but plain. Slaves were housed within large tenement blocks, similar to those in Rome and other cities but cleverly designed to be all but invisible from the high status buildings within the complex and from the roads passing through it. Slaves and other staff could pass from their residential quarters to other parts of the complex via a system of underground passages, so important visitors could enjoy the villa's many attractions while all maintenance work took place invisibly behind the scenes.

The villa complex featured an astonishing variety of buildings ranging from the traditional to outrageously modern, experimental styles employing new building techniques and materials. The use of new concrete technology enabled the construction of large curved structures and domed or vaulted roofs; the villa's roofscape thus presented a novel combination of angular and curvilinear forms. At ground level the mix of circular and rectilinear buildings offered a new architectural experience for people wandering amongst them. In several places, buildings seem to have been carefully located to enjoy stunning views of the villa's beautifully landscaped gardens and the mountains beyond. Within the grounds, water was channelled from the south-east via a complex system of aqueducts and pipes to serve the buildings along with numerous pools, fountains and other water features, before draining away northwards to the River Aniene. This water was also used to irrigate the villa's lush gardens, some of which were presumably used for the production of fruit and vegetables, while others were primarily ornamental.

The villa was furnished with hundreds of magnificent statues and other works of art of the highest quality. The statues included copies of ancient Greek and Egyptian masterpieces, as well as representations of Hadrian, other members of the imperial family, traditional Roman gods, and Antinous (Hadrian's young lover, who, as we will see shortly, was himself transformed into a god). Most of the statues were made locally of Italian marble, possibly at workshops within the villa complex, but, intriguingly, it seems that a few may have been already ancient originals imported form Egypt, Greece or elsewhere. Hadrian may well have regarded the conservation and presentation of these as important in the same way as he clearly valued ancient buildings and historic monuments, ordering repairs to many during his travels throughout the empire.

The villa was a private imperial residence, but was also much used for government business and thus regularly visited by important delegations from Rome and more distant places throughout the empire. While it is difficult to be sure in most cases exactly what individual rooms were used for, grand audience and dining halls have been identified in some places, with offices elsewhere. Clearly, groups of important guests met here and dined in the presence of Hadrian, when discourse no doubt ranged from the trivial to crucial matters of state, not to mention philosophical debate. Hadrian, we know, was particularly fond of dinner parties, a fact reflected in the splendid open-air dining areas recorded at Tivoli.

The effect this new villa had on visitors from far and wide must have been profound. It sought to impress in an innovative and, to the modern eye, very pleasing manner, in marked contrast to conventional Roman architecture which sought to impress through sheer scale and the regular repetition of established patterns. As Thorsten Opper eloquently observes, the villa 'expressed the invigorating vision of a brighter, freer world. While its buildings were certainly meant to impress, they do so through an almost playful monumentality that celebrates the limitless creativity of the human spirit rather than through sheer scale and the endless repetition of dominating blocks.'

As noted above, the entire complex seems to have developed around an initial blueprint, and this can only have been dreamed up by someone with an intuitive understanding of the power of architecture. That someone must surely have been Hadrian, the only individual with the power and resources to transform such an outrageous blueprint into extraordinary reality, and thus to have had a reason to dream it up in the first place. The entire complex is so astonishingly different from anything else that it must be regarded as something of a grand architectural experiment and, although Hadrian will have had a number of the best architects at his beck and call to help realise his vision, the fact that it is generally regarded today as an architectural triumph would seem to reflect favourably on his personal competence as a radical architect.

Inspecting the empire, AD 121-125

As we have already seen, Hadrian was widely travelled prior to becoming emperor. As emperor, he was to undertake three great journeys, inspecting all corners of the empire and visiting most if not all of the empire's 44 provinces. Surviving records of his travels are fragmentary, but we can recreate much from ancient texts along with inscriptions and coins from many different locations.

Hadrian's first great journey, which kept him away from Rome for four years, began in 121. He travelled initially to Gaul, and from there to Germania, where he had been stationed some twenty years previously. Here, he inspected Trajan's *limes* – the line of forts, fortlets and watchtowers that closed the gap between the two great rivers, the Rhine and the Danube, that formed much of the empire's eastern frontier. This frontier ran all the way from the North Sea to the Black Sea, but did not necessarily mark the 'edge of empire', as areas east of it, while not directly administered by Rome, were occupied by client kingdoms or groups tied to Rome by various treaties and agreements. The frontiers were porous, with much traffic passing in both directions, supposedly under the watchful eyes of border guards. Hadrian was not content with this arrangement, and ordered the construction of a continuous timber palisade along the entire 350 mile length of the *limes*. This was clearly part of his masterplan to consolidate the frontiers, enabling more efficient customs and immigration controls.

Although, unlike so many of his predecessors, he sought peace rather than war, Hadrian continued to place great emphasis on military training and discipline so that the army would be ready for action at any point. Despite his insistence on discipline, Hadrian was greatly respected by the troops as he ordered improvements in arms and equipment and led very much by personal example, often eating standard army rations, wearing a standard uniform and marching with the troops in full armour. Some 400,000 troops, to a man loyal to their 'commander-in-chief', were stationed largely around the fringes of the empire, enabling an estimated 60 million people to live within the empire, largely in peace, throughout Hadrian's reign. The unqualified support of the military owed much to Hadrian's reputation as a soldier; a reputation of which he was justifiably proud.

After leaving the Rhineland, Hadrian moved on to Britain, bringing with him a new governor, his personal friend, Aulus Platorius Nepos. There had clearly been conflict in Britain prior to the imperial visit; although the nature of the problem is unclear it presumably involved incursions from the north, where Roman influence had been minimal for three decades. Hadrian's response was to build a mighty wall from the Tyne to the Solway (considered in detail in Chapters 2 and 3). We have no record of what Hadrian did while in Britain, but it is a safe bet that he would have personally inspected the frontier zone, probably riding and walking the wild, windswept hills of what was destined to become the Hadrian's Wall World Heritage Site.

It seems to have been while he was in Britain that Hadrian dismissed two of his senior officials for behaving in an 'unacceptably informal fashion' (frustratingly, no details are given) in the company of his wife, Sabina. The source of this story adds that Hadrian would also have liked to dismiss Sabina on account of her moody and difficult behaviour, but did not, probably due to the unsavoury publicity that such action would have caused. Bad feeling between the two was apparently mutual; Sabina is said to have ensured that she never fell pregnant because in her view any child of Hadrian's would have been harmful to the human race! As noted earlier, it is quite possible that the marriage was never even consummated, and given Hadrian's preference for sex with attractive young boys it is doubtful whether much hope ever existed for what we might regard as a conventional, loving marriage. We will have more to say about the emperor's love life shortly.

Hadrian did not linger long in Britain, perhaps staying only for a few weeks during the summer of 122 before crossing back to Gaul (where he erected a splendid basilica to the recently deceased Plotina in her home town of Nimes, and a tomb for his favourite horse, Borysthenes, at nearby Apt) then moving on to Spain. For unknown reasons he seems never to have returned to his home town of Italica, but did grant it 'colonia' status and had a magnificent theatre built for its people. He spent the winter at the historically important city of Tarraco (the oldest Roman foundation in Spain, dating back to 218 BC) where he convened a great assembly of officials from throughout the Spanish provinces. At Tarraco, he was attacked by an insane slave, but, rather than seek retribution (which he could instantly have administered) he insisted that the slave receive medical attention. This incident is said to have gained the emperor much respect and certainly shows a humane aspect to his nature, illustrating his stated view that the law should combine justice with human kindness. It is fascinating to note that 150 years previously, in January 27 BC, Hadrian's great role-model, Augustus, had officially become Rome's first emperor, before beginning a three-year tour of Gaul and Spain that saw him spend the winter of 27/26 BC at Tarraco. It is surely significant that Hadrian chose to spend this anniversary at Tarraco, marking it by rebuilding the city's Temple of Augustus and also by adopting a new title; previously, inscriptions on coins had read 'IMP. CAESAR TRAIANUS HADRIANUS AUG.', but from this point on they would read simply 'HADRIANUS AUGUSTUS'. Clearly, Hadrian saw himself, and wished others to see him, as a new Augustus.

Early in 123, Hadrian sailed from Spain to North Africa, where he personally led his troops against an uprising in the province of Mauretania. Within a few weeks he was on the move again, sailing eastwards the entire length of the Mediterranean to Antioch. From here, he travelled overland to the frontier on the Euphrates, holding talks with the Parthian king, Osroes, which seem not only to have averted possible conflict with the Parthians, but also ensured peace in this potentially volatile area for the rest of his reign. In holding these peace talks Hadrian was again following the example of Augustus who, one and a half centuries earlier, had himself sought to avert military conflict in Parthia through negotiation.

Hadrian then moved north to the Black Sea, stopping at Trapezus above the Black Sea coast to erect altars and a statue of himself at the site of a famous late fifth-century BC incident involving Xenophon, a heroic Athenian commander. This neatly illustrates his fascination with ancient Greek history. From here he sailed back westwards to Nicomedia, where he ordered large-scale rebuilding work following a catastrophic earthquake, then travelled overland to Ephesus. The logistics involved in transporting the imperial party from city to city and ensuring appropriate accommodation must have been daunting, but the emperor's desire to see everywhere for himself meant that the necessary arrangements were put place without question. During this tour he visited many cities and showered them with honours, ordering the construction of many wonderful new buildings and the restoration of others. Several cities were renamed in his honour, Hadrianopolis being a popular option. The emperor concerned himself closely with the administration of justice in the provinces, but also, no doubt, took an appropriate amount of time out for drinking and hunting.

It was probably about this time that a momentous event in Hadrian's life occurred: he met a beautiful Bithynian teenage boy who would soon be transformed into a god. This boy was Antinous, and we will consider his deification shortly; for now we must say something about the nature of his relationship with Hadrian. Roman society did not disapprove of homosexuality and we have already noted that Hadrian followed Trajan in preferring sex with young boys than with women. In Hadrian's mind, however, Antinous was much, much more than just another sexual play-thing. There has been much speculation about the nature of the relationship, but it is perhaps best regarded as a classic example of an idealised and highly respected form of Athenian homosexual relationship between an *erastes* ('lover') and his *eromenos* ('beloved'). In such relationships the *erastes* (Hadrian) oversaw the physical and moral development of the *eromenos* (Antinous), who could be expected to provide sexual gratification in return. Such relationships were not simply about sex, but could involve genuine affection and passion between partners. Problems could arise as the younger partner achieved manhood, but, as we will see shortly, Hadrian and Antinous would be spectacularly deprived of the opportunity to develop their relationship past this stage.

Continuing his tour, Hadrian crossed briefly to Europe to the province of Thrace, then sailed back to Asia to inspect Mysia. Again demonstrating his fascination with history, he visited the site of the Battle of Granicus, at which Alexander the Great had won a famous victory in 334 BC. While visiting Troy he ordered the restoration of the tomb of the famous Greek warrior, Ajax; another example of his interest in the conservation of what we classify today, rather abstractly, as 'ancient monuments' but which, to him, were tangible indicators of a heroic past with which he sought to demonstrate a direct link.

Hadrian now headed back to Athens, sailing via Rhodes where he apparently ordered the rebuilding of the Colossus, felled in an earthquake three centuries earlier. Sadly, for reasons unknown, this was an architectural project that never came to fruition. In late summer 124, he arrived in Athens, to which he must have longed to return ever since his earlier visit a dozen years previously. The six months he now spent here were extraordinary. Soon after arriving he was inaugurated into the category of *mustae* (novices), enabling him to participate in the Eleusinian Mysteries, an ancient annual ceremony linked to the mysteries of life, death and rebirth, open to all Greek speaking people. This was clearly the kind of ceremony that appealed to Hadrian's interests in the metaphysical. After several days of preparation, the culmination of the Mysteries took place within a great building known as the Telesterion at Eleusis, 20km west of Athens. The details of the ceremony were a closely guarded secret, but they probably involved the taking of a hallucinogenic drink and apparently culminated in a revelation about life after death. Many *mustae* returned to take part in the Mysteries in future years, as experienced participants known as *epoptai*, as Hadrian would do four years later.

During his stay in Athens he revised the law, modified the economy, ordered the construction of several new public buildings, and began the construction of a new residential district to be known as Hadrianopolis. A great entrance arch to this new district survives today; on its west face (facing the Acropolis) an inscription reads 'This is Athens the old city of Thesius' whereas the east face states 'This is the city of Hadrian, not of Thesius' (Thesius was the mythological founder of Athens). Within Hadrianopolis district, Hadrian ordered the completion of the vast temple to Zeus Olympios (hitherto unfinished despite sporadic phases of construction stretching back over seven centuries) as a project to help unite the people and to cement the position of Athens as the spiritual centre of the civilised world. Another ambitious building project was the 'Library of Hadrian', a cultural centre for the city with 100 marble columns and gilded roofs. The Athenians, apparently out of genuine affection as well as political prudence, placed a statue of Hadrian in their most sacred of places, the Parthenon of Athena. Hadrian travelled throughout the Peloponnese over the winter of 124/5, visiting many famous places including Sparta, Corinth and the ruins of Mycaenae. During his travels he ordered many more construction projects including the restoration of the already 500 year-old gold and ivory statue of Zeus at the ancient Greek sanctuary of Olympia. In March 125 he was back in Athens for the festival of Dionysos, which he had previously attended before becoming emperor back in 112. This time, in traditional Greek costume and to the hearty approval of the locals, he served as president of the festival. He eventually set sail from Athens in Spring 125, visiting the Oracle of Apollo at Delphi before sailing on to Rome via Sicily, where he observed the sunrise from the summit of Mount Etna.

Home in Rome, AD 125-128

Back in Rome, Hadrian had much to do, but what must have pleased him most was to see the progress with his various architectural projects. The magnificent Pantheon was now complete, and he held court within it. Nearby, the splendid temple to the deified Trajan and Plotina was also complete. At the heart of the city, work on the enormous Temple of Venus and Roma was presumably now under way. Work on the vast imperial villa at Tivoli must still have been very much in progress, but many buildings here must now have been complete so that Hadrian could reside and work here, rather than in the city, as he wished. Work on the great mausoleum and the associated bridge (the *Pons Aelius*) was presumably also well underway, though this would not see completion within Hadrian's lifetime.

Alongside his love of Greece, Hadrian also had great respect for the traditions and values of Rome and Italy. Amongst his political reforms was the division of Italy into four new regions, but this arrangement proved unpopular and was later abandoned. In August 127, lavish entertainment was laid on for the people of Rome to celebrate Hadrian's tenth anniversary as emperor. In 128, the increasingly popular emperor finally accepted the Senate's offer of the prestigious title *Pater Patriae* (Father of the People); just like Augustus, Hadrian accepted this honour at the third time of asking, whereas most of his predecessors had simply assumed it upon their accession.

An African summer, AD 128

After three years in Rome Hadrian was off on his travels once again, this time to Africa, where his arrival coincided with the first rainfall in five years, bringing a welcome end to a serious drought. As with previous tours, grand new buildings were lavished on numerous towns, some of which (including Carthage) renamed themselves Hadrianopolis in honour of their emperor. He further enhanced his popularity amongst the masses by insisting on fair treatment for peasants and giving tax breaks for some agricultural operations. In July 128, he addressed the troops at Lambaesis, where the sole legion in Africa (*III Augusta*) was based, and some of his words were engraved onto the base of a memorial column, erected on the parade ground as a permanent record of the imperial visit. Today, these inscriptions survive as the only contemporary and undeniably authentic record of an address by a Roman emperor to his troops. As a military man, Hadrian was in his element here, and the surviving inscription records that he offered congratulations on construction work and military exercises, while providing some learned advice on cavalry manoeuvres. Although detailed evidence is lacking, we can imagine the emperor making similar inspections and offering such words of encouragement and advice to troops throughout the empire. Hadrian had no desire to send his army to war, but his troops were well trained, enthusiastic, loyal and constantly ready for action if required. Dio, writing a century later, observes:

'Both by his example and by his precepts he so trained and disciplined the whole military force throughout the entire empire that even today the methods then introduced by him are the soldiers' law of campaigning. This best explains why he lived for the most part at peace with foreign nations.'

The construction of a military barrier along the entire northern fringe of the Atlas Mountains and Sahara Desert would have been absurd, but Hadrian does seem to have ordered the building of some lengths of frontier wall along the empire's southern boundary. Known as the *Fossatum Africae*, some stretches of this survive in Algeria, Tunisia and Morocco. Although essentially a ditch with earthen embankments, supplemented in places with walls of stone or mud-brick, this does seem to have incorporated fortlets and turrets in a similar arrangement to the British frontier, and thus to have been about controlling rather than excluding movement across it. The aim may have been to exercise control over nomadic people south of the new barrier, while incorporating into the empire the more fertile land, and permanent settlements, to its north. Tantalisingly, Hadrian's speeches to the troops at Lambaesis include praise for the Second Cohort of Spaniards for their 'skill in building a wall and digging a ditch'. Could these men have been involved in the construction of a frontier wall at the opposite extremity of the empire from Hadrian's Wall? The detailed chronology and purpose of the *Fossatum Africae* demand much further study, but it certainly appears probable on the basis of currently available evidence that Hadrian did indeed initiate some form of architectural barrier along parts of the African frontier.

Athens, the East and Egypt, AD 128-132

Hadrian returned to Rome after his African trip, but within a few weeks, in September 128, he was off again for another six-month stay in Athens, where construction work on the fabulous new buildings ordered during the previous imperial visit was now well underway. He again took part in the Mysteries of Eleusis, this time amongst the *epoptai* (those who had already attended at least once before, as he had done in 124). As noted earlier, the exact nature of this ceremony was (and remains to this day) a well-kept secret, known only to its participants, but it seems again to have had a profound effect on Hadrian, playing on his well-known fascination for the occult and astrology. Hadrian had been ill earlier in the year and his thoughts may well have turned to his own mortality, but after the festival at Eleusis a coin was issued announcing to the world that the emperor had been 'reborn'. The Greeks (who had a long-established tradition of regarding their most distinguished leaders as gods within their lifetimes, in contrast to Rome where emperors were generally deified posthumously) seem to have increasingly regarded Hadrian as a god from this point, identifying him closely with Zeus. Hadrian's personal views on his Greek deification are not recorded, but he seems to have offered no resistance to the trend so we may assume that he found it to his liking.

In the spring of 129 Hadrian, presumably now constantly accompanied by Antinous, crossed the Adriatic to Ephesus to begin a two-year inspection of the eastern provinces. He was welcomed amidst great public acclaim at Ephesus and many other cities, and substantial new buildings and other gifts were granted to the people almost everywhere the imperial party went. The people responded by erecting numerous magnificent statues to their emperor in temples and at other public places. On the eastern frontier Hadrian undertook further discussions with the Parthians to reinforce the peace negotiated six years earlier; Parthia remained a potentially hostile and serious adversary, but Hadrian's tactic of defending the frontier through negotiation rather than conflict seems to have succeeded.

In 130, Hadrian arrived in the ancient Jewish city of Jerusalem and ordered its transformation into a Roman colony, to be known as *Aelia Capitolina* (in honour of Jupiter Capitolinus, greatest of the Roman gods, often equated with Zeus). In addition to banning them from the city, he also withdrew certain political privileges from the Jews and banned circumcision. The ancient temple, traditionally the centre of the Jewish world but in ruins since its destruction by Rome back in 71, was replaced with a magnificent new temple to Jupiter Capitolinus, and a large statue of a sow, offensive to Jews and illustrative of Roman domination, was displayed at one of the city's main gates. Exactly why the previously tolerant Hadrian made these clearly provocative decisions is not recorded, but the explanation probably lies in a combination of his obsessive Hellenism, with which Judaism was clearly incompatible, and a desire to reduce the political influence of Jewish leaders who had the potential to encourage serious rebellions in Judaea and elsewhere. Before long (as we will see shortly) these decisions would cause Rome much grief.

Hadrian moved on from Jerusalem to Egypt where he was no doubt eager to explore aspects of ancient Egyptian culture for himself. On the road to Egypt he paused at Pelusium to oversee conservation work at the tomb of Pompey the Great, murdered here in 48 BC. This provides yet another example of Hadrian's interest in the past and his desire to preserve significant ancient monuments for the future. The imperial party then moved on to Alexandria, a great trading city and centre of learning with a famous library. Hadrian paid due homage at the tomb of Alexander the Great, and promoted the worship of the Alexandrian god, Serapis, alongside that of Jupiter and Zeus. These were popular moves, but the locals regarded his creation of a chapel to himself within the Serapeum of Alexandria as arrogant. Despite official acceptance, the Alexandrians seem not to have taken to Hadrian with the same degree of adoration as other Greek colonies; he seems even to have been regarded by some as a figure of ridicule. He fancied himself as a poet, an orator and a philosopher, but, although he perhaps failed to recognise it, was out of his depth within the academic environment of Alexandria. However, his generous sponsorship of the arts (coupled with observation of one academic that it would perhaps be unwise to fall out with the commander of thirty legions!) meant that academics tended to avoid serious argument with him.

Perhaps as welcome relief from the academic world of Alexandria, Hadrian and Antinous seem to have spent some time at the nearby resort of Canopus, renowned for its 'extreme licentiousness'. Hadrian apparently enjoyed his time here, as Canopus would find itself commemorated in the form of a beautiful pool surrounded by colonnades and exquisite statues within the architecture of the imperial villa at Tivoli. Further relief from academic debate was provided in the form of a great lion hunt in the adjacent province of Cyrenaica, during which Hadrian is said to have killed a ferocious lion that was attacking Antinous. Hadrian's passion for hunting is reflected in a series of circular sculptures ('tondi') now incorporated within the Arch of Constantine in Rome. These must originally have formed part of a great hunting monument, the form of which is unknown. One of the tondi depicts a lion hunt and may even record the above-mentioned hunt in particular. Unfortunately, several of the figures have had their faces reworked, so we cannot be certain how many of them were originally of Hadrian or Antinous.

Before long, it was time for the imperial party to set off up the Nile, as so many tourists continue to do today, in search of the wonders of ancient Egypt.

Egypt was a crucially important Roman province, as the fertile floodplains of the Nile provided a reliable and abundant annual harvest, produce from which was distributed to cities around the Mediterranean. Although Greek was the language of government in Egypt, the peasant masses remained loyal to Egyptian tradition, and the ancient gods were still worshipped at many great temples along the Nile. Something of the awesome power of ancient Egyptian religion can still be experienced by the modern tourist at the ruins of Thebes (Luxor) and other places, and we may well wonder how these places, then still served by priests and in regular religious use, would have affected Hadrian, especially as Roman emperors were widely regarded as the successors of the ancient pharaohs as both kings and gods. Ancient sources record that Hadrian discussed sacred rites and spells with an Egyptian priest and magician named Pachrates, and that he was so impressed that he paid double the usual fee for his consultation. The imperial party then moved on to inspect the pyramids and Great Sphinx at Giza, the symbolic architecture of which must have left Hadrian entranced.

However, all was not well in Egypt at this time. Whereas Hadrian's previous arrival in Africa, a couple of years earlier, had coincided with rainfall that ended a five-year drought, his visit to Egypt occurred at a time when the Nile floods had largely failed for a second consecutive year. Despite his now divine status, Hadrian was powerless to do anything about the consequent crop failures which would have serious repercussions throughout the empire as the usual Egyptian grain supplies failed to arrive. Regardless of its impact elsewhere, such crop failure was a disaster within Egypt, and would have resulted in widespread famine. All in all, this was not a good time for Hadrian to be visiting, but it was about to get a great deal worse.

In October 130, in circumstances that will remain forever mysterious and which have given rise to much intriguing speculation, Antinous (quite possibly the only person with whom Hadrian was ever truly in love) drowned in the Nile. It is possible that this was a simple accident, but several factors point towards some kind of ritual death, perhaps even suicide. We have commented earlier on Hadrian's interest in the occult, and on the value he attached to spiritual matters, as exemplified by his fascination with the Mysteries of Eleusis and his consultation with Pachrates. Antinous, we may assume, had similar interests. The Nile had long been associated with sacrificial drownings, with special funeral proceedings and sometimes even deification reserved for those who drowned within it. Osiris, the Egyptian god of the underworld, had drowned within its waters and Antinous died in late October, quite possibly on 24th October, the very day of the traditional commemoration of the death of Osiris.

The place of Antinous' death may also be of significance: Hermopolis Major (360 miles upriver from the mouth of the Nile) contained the main shrine of Thoth, the Egyptian god of knowledge and philosophy, whose remit included magic and astrology. Perhaps Antinous, acting on information provided by local Egyptian priests, and possibly without Hadrian's knowledge, willingly sacrificed himself in the belief that by doing so he would ensure longer life for his beloved emperor. Intriguingly, if Hadrian and Antinous did regard themselves as *erastes* and *eromenos* (as discussed above), then the latter's death removed the risk of complications that could have developed as he moved into full adulthood. We will never know for certain what happened, but Hadrian was heartbroken; we are told that he 'wept like a woman'. Although Antinous had played no significant role in public life, other than as the emperor's personal partner, in death he was deified and shrines to him were set up all over the empire. Hadrian did not insist on the worship of Antinous, but, nevertheless, his cult became extraordinarily popular, rivalling that of Christ; hundreds of beautiful statues were sculpted, and his image appeared on thousands of coins and other objects. One extraordinary Greek statue depicts Hadrian wearing a breastplate embellished with an image of Antinous in place of the usual mythical Gorgon, Medusa, traditionally worn to help ward off evil. Whether Hadrian actually owned such a breastplate, and, if so, what his exact thoughts were in replacing Medusa with Antinous, are unknown. The favoured image of Antinous, surely authorised by Hadrian, was of striking melancholy beauty and perhaps illustrates a melancholy aspect to Hadrian's character. Today, nineteen centuries after his death, Antinous remains one of the most instantly recognisable and widely reproduced figures from the ancient world, an extraordinary result for one whose sole known achievement in life was to be chosen as an emperor's boyfriend.

Hadrian ordered the construction of a magnificent new Hellenistic city, Antinoopolis, on the bank of the Nile close to the spot where Antinous died. This had a reputation for miracles and magic and became a great pilgrimage centre; people came from far and wide to worship the 'great God Osirisantinous'. It was also famous for its annual games, the *Antinoeia*, which offered substantial prizes and attracted top-quality entrants to its music and art festivals as well as its athletic and equestrian competitions. Spectacular ruins of Antinoopolis stood into the early nineteenth century, when, appallingly, they were systematically destroyed in the name of agricultural development; much masonry was recycled in the construction of a nearby sugar factory, roads and a dam, while marble and limestone monuments were crushed to produce lime.

The reasons for the popularity of Antinous' cult are complex and cannot concern us here, but we should note that his death had a profound impact on Hadrian, whose subsequent demeanour and decision-making seem to have been clouded by the loss of his young lover. Despite his grief, however, he succeeded in creating triumph from tragedy: he created arguably the last great pagan god of the classical world whose cult represented a unifying force in Rome, Greece and Egypt, proving immensely popular throughout much of the Mediterranean and beyond.

After the death of Antinous, Hadrian remained at Hermopolis for several months before continuing up the Nile to Thebes, where, in spite of his raw grief, he must have been enthralled by the vast Temple of Karnak, the numerous other magnificent temples, and the Valley of the Kings. He eventually left Egypt in 131, travelling back through Jerusalem where he presumably spent time inspecting his 'new' city, *Aelia Capitolina*. The detailed chronology of his decisions regarding the future of Jerusalem is not clear; some were apparently made during his visit in 130, while others may date from a year later. Whatever the detailed timing, his already ruthless attitude towards the Jews may have been hardened still further by his loss of Antinous; in Hadrian's mind, Greco-Roman unity, as represented by the emperor himself alongside Zeus, Jupiter and Antinous, would triumph over the Jews whatever the cost.

Hadrian continued his homeward journey in familiar fashion, visiting numerous towns and cities, founding monuments and distributing gifts as he went, eventually arriving back at Ephesus where he must have been impressed by a beautiful new temple dedicated to him. From Ephesus, the imperial party set sail across the Aegean back to Athens.

Back in Athens, Hadrian did much to promote the cult of Antinous but did not shrink from other duties. He inspected his new district of Hadrianopolis, including the magnificent Olympeion (the temple of Olympian Zeus) which was dedicated amongst great festivity even though building work was not yet quite complete. This vast new temple, with 104 columns, was decorated with numerous statues of Hadrian presented by various Greek cities; today's dramatic ruins give a flavour of what must have been a truly awe-inspiring monument. The magnificent Library of Hadrian may also have been open by this time, and we can imagine the emperor inspecting the building and its contents with great pride. It may have been now that Hadrian initiated the setting up of the Panhellenion, a spiritual and cultural union of Greek city-states centred on Athens (though ultimately subservient to the Emperor of Rome). Hadrian's concept of the Panhellenion was inspired by Pericles, undisputed leader of the Athenians half a millennium earlier, who had attempted something similar but failed due to opposition from Sparta, then Athens' main military rival. Five centuries later,

Hadrian went out of his way to ensure the Spartans were fully on board. Athens was now a truly magnificent cultural metropolis at the spiritual heart of the empire, and Hadrian must surely have intended to return before long. This, however, was destined to be his final visit to his beloved Greece.

War in Judaea, AD 132-135

Hadrian's movements in 132-135 are not well recorded. He probably spent most of this period back in Rome, where he would have enjoyed organising the development of his sumptuous villa at Tivoli. Remarkably, archaeologists have recently discovered a sanctuary to Antinous (the *Antinoeion*) adjacent to a main entrance route into the villa complex, and there are sound reasons for believing that this may have included Antinous' tomb; doubtless Hadrian was its architect, as he was the architect of the entire Antinous cult. The splendid obelisk, inscribed with hieroglyphic script, now standing on the Pincio Hill in central Rome seems originally to have been part of the *Antinoeion*. During this period, Hadrian seems also to have spent some time on campaign with the army in Judaea where a major Jewish revolt had to be dealt with by military force. This Jewish War, although arising out of long standing animosity between Rome and Jerusalem, was undeniably precipitated by Hadrian's earlier banning of circumcision and the rebranding of Jerusalem as *Aelia Capitolina*. It became by far the most bloody conflict of his reign, involving perhaps as many as a dozen legions engaged not in great set-piece battles of the type on which the Roman army thrived, but in a seemingly interminable number of small-scale skirmishes against a well-organised enemy of 'freedom-fighters' practicing a form of guerrilla warfare within their own homeland.

At the beginning of the Jewish conflict, in 132, Hadrian ordered Sextus Julius Severus, the governor of Britain, to cross to the opposite extremity of the empire and take command of the Roman forces. This is interesting as it demonstrates not only that a highly regarded general could be moved around the empire at the emperor's behest, but also that a man of such standing had been in charge of Britain. We don't know anything for sure about the nature or scale of conflict in Britain under Hadrian, but the fact that Julius Severus was chosen, above all others, to take charge in Judaea perhaps suggests that the British 'enemy' may have practiced similar tactics to the Jews, and that it was his specific experience in dealing with this that led to his transfer.

Contemporary sources record that more than half a million Jewish men were killed in military action, and more than a thousand towns and villages destroyed by Roman troops. Untold numbers of non-combatants, including women and children, also lost their lives through a combination of direct Roman military action, disease and famine. Roman losses were also significant, with tens of thousands of casualties apparently including the entire 5,000-strong 22nd Legion. The revolt was eventually over by 135, after which the province of Judaea was merged with Galilee and renamed Syria-Palaestina. Hadrian had achieved his aim of crushing the Jews, to whom he would henceforth be known as 'Hadrian the wicked'. Early in his reign, Hadrian had earned much respect amongst Jews for the fair manner in which he had dealt with matters in Egypt following a Jewish rebellion there, but from now on every mention of his name in Jewish circles would be followed by the Hebrew curse 'may his bones rot'.

With the possible exception of a war in Britain early in his reign, about which little is known, this was Hadrian's sole large-scale conflict throughout his entire reign. Significantly it was not about conquering enemy territory, or defeating an invading army, but was an internal conflict, fought entirely within the bounds of the empire against 'an enemy within'. Following victory, Hadrian was proclaimed *'imperator'* by the army for the second time (the previous occasion was on his accession rather than in response to any particular military campaign). The senior officers who masterminded the campaign, including Julius Severus, received an honorary triumph (*triumphalia ornamenta*), the highest possible military honour, while numerous lower ranking soldiers received awards for valour (*dona militaria*). Commemorative monuments were erected within Syria-Palaestina and in Rome, but the emperor did not glory in the victory; he did not hold any kind of triumph back in Rome as his predecessors would have done, and there was no issue of triumphal coinage. He seems to have regarded the war as a necessary evil to defeat the Jews and enable the development of a peaceful Hellenistic province. In the longer term, however, this aspiration proved somewhat over ambitious, and the region remains a hotbed of religious and political turmoil to this day.

The succession crisis, AD 137-138

After the Jewish War, Hadrian, possibly now in poor health, returned to Rome. As his health declined, he had to think seriously about his successor. His ninety-year-old and very distinguished brother-in-law, Julius Servianus (who two decades earlier had been a contender to succeed Trajan), and his now-deceased sister, Domitia Paulina, had an eighteen year-old grandson, Pedanius Fuscus, now his closest living male relative and thus a potential successor. However, Hadrian was not overly fond of his sister's family and chose to overlook his young great-nephew. Instead, in the year 136, he made a surprise and much ridiculed decision to adopt Lucius Ceionius Commodus, who took the name Lucius Aelius Caesar. Aelius Caesar's greatest attribute was said to be his good looks, and rumours circulated about the nature of his relationship with the emperor. Despite such tittle-tattle, Hadrian's motives were almost certainly well-founded, with the empire's long-term future very much in mind. One of Aelius Caesar's daughters was betrothed to Marcus Annius Verus, a young man of whom Hadrian was very fond, referring to him as 'Verissimus' ('the sincerest' or 'the truest'). He had a Spanish father and may have been distantly related to Hadrian, although this cannot be proved. Hadrian granted the young Marcus Annius Verus important positions, suggesting that he may have been grooming him as an eventual successor, but he was not yet old enough to become emperor. Perhaps, therefore, Lucius Aelius Caesar was seen in Hadrian's mind as no more than a stopgap, a suggestion supported by the fact that he was known to be in poor health.

In 137, Pedanius Fuscus was executed and the aged Julius Servianus forced to commit suicide, presumably because they were thought by Hadrian to have tried to organise some kind of coup. Just prior to his death, Servianus attempted revenge on Hadrian, praying to the gods that the ailing emperor would 'long for death, yet be unable to die'. The same year saw the death of Sabina, but allegations she was poisoned by order of Hadrian have no foundation. Despite their apparently loveless marriage, Hadrian generally treated his wife with respect and after her death he demanded her deification, which the Senate approved.

Plans for the succession were thrown into chaos in January 138 when the sick Lucius Aelius Caesar dropped dead. Hadrian announced an alternative plan on his 62nd birthday, 24th January 138; he now adopted his trusted advisor Titus Aurelius Fulvus Boionius Arrius Antoninus, who happened to be an uncle of Marcus Annius Verus. This was on the condition that Antoninus jointly adopted Lucius Ceionius Commodus (son of the recently deceased Aelius Caesar; now generally known as Lucius Verus) and Marcus Annius Verus as his own eventual successors. Despite Hadrian's ailing condition, this was a masterstroke that ensured sound leadership for the empire for four decades after his death. It seems that his aim all along may have been to ensure the young 'Verissimus', now known to history as the great philosopher-emperor Marcus Aurelius, would eventually succeed him. It is also interesting to note that in seeking to ensure two generations of successors Hadrian was following the example of Augustus, his great role model in so many things.

A cruel end, AD 138

Hadrian became increasingly paranoid and vindictive as his health declined, allegedly ordering the deaths of several loyal colleagues whom he regarded as possible opponents. It is not possible to diagnose his final illness with certainty, but attention has recently been drawn to the unusual creases in his earlobes, distinctive features of many statues, that might be indicative of coronary artery disease. He ordered a slave to stab him to death, but the slave refused. He then ordered his doctor to poison him, but the doctor opted to commit suicide rather than murder his emperor. Whatever the nature of his condition, it was clearly very unpleasant; Servianus' prayer, it would seem, was being answered by the gods.

Hadrian moved to the coast for his final days, dying at Baiae near Naples on 10th July 138. His final melancholy and rather moving poem (which, it has to be said, defies effective translation into English) was addressed to his own restless soul:

Little spirit, gentle and wandering,
Body's companion and guest,
To what places now will you take flight,
Pale, stark and bare,
Unable, as you used, to play?

As we have seen, many people regarded Hadrian as a god during his lifetime. It was traditional practice, however, for Roman emperors to be deified only after death. Due to his unpopularity within the Senate at the end of his life, there was much opposition to Hadrian's deification, but his successor, Antoninus, ensured that the necessary procedures were completed so that he officially became a god. Hadrian's deification ceremony in Rome must have been a magnificent spectacle, witnessed by tens of thousands and commemorated on gold coins showing his soul being flown up to the heavens on a great eagle. His ashes, initially buried at Baiae, were interred in 139, along with those of Sabina and Lucius Aelius Caesar, within his vast new mausoleum (where they presumably remained until the building was looted by Visigoths during Alaric's sacking of Rome in 410). Within Rome, in addition to dedicating the new imperial mausoleum to Hadrian and Sabina, Antoninus built a splendid temple to the deified Hadrian and instituted a quinquennial festival to maintain his significance within the collective consciousness of the people. The loyal Antoninus had been present at Hadrian's death, and his great loyalty to his predecessor earned him the epithet 'Pius'; thus he is known to history as Antoninus Pius.

Summary

The *Historia Augusta* records that Hadrian died *'invisus omnibus'*, usually translated as 'hated by all' (although we should note it can also be translated rather less dramatically as 'unseen by all' - typically of Hadrian, even in death alternative interpretations are possible). Similarly, Cassius Dio states that Hadrian was hated by the people at the time of his death, noting that this was specifically 'on account of the murders committed at the start and end of his reign'. Given that his lengthy reign was generally peaceful and prosperous, it is perhaps surprising that he should have been universally hated at the time of his death; it may be that this statement is simply not true. The circumstances of his accession, and the lingering doubt that the whole process had been stage-managed by Trajan's wife, certainly did not endear him to many, while the executions of prominent potential opponents following his accession and towards the end of his life rendered him unpopular within the Senate, despite his protestations of innocence. His campaign of non-aggression must have generated some opposition, as individual commanders and the empire as a whole were denied potential glory through military conquest. We may assume, however, that many within the military were grateful for the fact that they were not called upon to lay down their lives campaigning for sovereignty over some far-distant land in which they had no personal interest, and we should recall that Hadrian enjoyed great respect from his fellow soldiers when out in the field and never faced even a hint of military rebellion throughout the entire two decades of his reign. We should also note that he could be ruthless when he deemed such an approach necessary, as illustrated by his vicious and ultimately victorious campaign against the Jews.

Hadrian had great respect for the past. His interest in visiting (and often restoring) ancient sites and monuments would, in more recent times, have qualified him as an antiquarian; he would, without doubt, be pleased to see the effort and expense poured into the study and conservation of his various architectural projects today. He was a great respecter of important historical figures, in particular Augustus, Rome's revered first emperor, on whom he clearly tried to model himself in certain ways. For example, he followed Augustus, in believing that the eastern limits of the empire should extend no further than the natural boundaries of the Rhine, Danube and Euphrates. He also desired to follow Augustus in ruling as a 'first amongst equals', as a representative of the people, rather than as any kind of dictator. He seems to have had a genuine interest in the lives of the common people, passing laws in their favour and doing all he could to improve the lot of men serving within the army. His decision to define and consolidate the empire's frontiers, after the aggressive expansionism of Trajan, was perhaps inevitable, but certainly led to a period of sustained prosperity for those living within the empire.

Hadrian's biographers tell many stories about him and, while the authenticity of some may be open to question, collectively they offer an intriguing insight into his character. Some stress his dealings with ordinary people. In one, a woman attempts to ask him a question as he passes by, to which he replies that he does not have time; 'then cease being emperor', she chastises him, whereupon he stops, turns back and listens to what she has to say. Various confrontations between modern day politicians and 'everyday folk', often rather poorly managed, come readily to mind by way of comparison. On another occasion he was attacked by a mad slave who tried to stab him; his commendable response was to order medical treatment for the man's condition.

Hadrian, it seems, was not without a sense of humour. One amusing tale relates that he often used public baths and on one such occasion recognised an old military colleague who was rubbing his body against a wall; the veteran explained that he had fallen on hard times and could not afford a slave to rub his body so used the wall of the baths instead. Hadrian immediately gifted him some slaves together with the cost of their maintenance. On a later occasion, he witnessed a number of men rubbing their bodies against the wall in the hope that their emperor would be in similarly generous mood. Instead he called them out in pairs and ordered them to rub each other! Another story relates to his amazing ability never to forget a face. He had refused a request to a grey-haired man, only for the same man to return later with died hair to ask again; rather than admonish the man, whom he recognised instantly despite the change in hair colour, Hadrian simply commented 'I have already refused this to your father!'

Another oft-quoted example of his humour comes in the form of a brief verse sent to his friend, the writer and poet Publius Annius Florus. At about the time Hadrian was in Britain, Florus sent him a short poem reflecting that he preferred his life in Rome to that of his restless emperor travelling the northern provinces:

> *I don't want to be Caesar, please,*
> *To tramp round the Britons, weak at the knees,*
> *[one line lost]*
> *In the Scythian frosts to freeze.*

Hadrian replied:

> *I don't want to be Florus, please,*
> *To tramp round pubs, into bars to squeeze,*
> *To lurk about eating pies and peas,*
> *To get myself infested with fleas.*

Even allowing for the fact that such verses inevitably lose something in translation from their original Latin (these translations are provided by Anthony Birley), it would be fair to say that this effort would not win any poetry competitions in the ancient or modern worlds. It does, however, provide a fascinating contrast to his rather more profound final verse (quoted earlier), and certainly suggests that he enjoyed such banter, presumably a welcome distraction from the incessant formal correspondence to which he must have had to allocate much time on his travels.

Despite such frivolities, Hadrian took the management of the empire very seriously, taking a keen personal interest in mundane aspects of government to which other emperors paid little attention. The *Historia Augusta* records that 'he had as complete a knowledge of the state budget in all its details as any careful householder has of his own household'. He wrote his own speeches and played a personal role in the development of a range of new laws, including some designed specifically to improve the lives of slaves. He introduced a law on treasure trove, stating that the value of a find should be shared equally between finder and landowner; the same condition exists within our present-day Treasure Act, and has been applied in recent years to several spectacular finds of Roman date, not least the Staffordshire Moorlands Pan (discussed in Chapter 3). He would have enjoyed seeing his own law applied to 'treasure' bearing his own name, but what he would have made of the little pan being valued at £100,000 is anybody's guess.

Hadrian admired the political, military and religious traditions of Rome, but his mind, imagination and spirit were very much Greek. Within the empire he sought the establishment of a great 'Graeco-Roman' civilisation, but also embraced a degree of regional diversity, for example in religion, as long as this did not conflict with Graeco-Roman tradition. One of the key aspects of Hadrian's empire, that helped to bind it together, was the emperor himself. Hadrian championed the cult of the emperor, regarding himself as a unifying force around which everyone could rally.

He was passionate about the arts, including literature and music, but in particular high quality architecture on a grand scale. He sought opportunities to exercise his passion for architecture everywhere he went. His tragic loss of Antinous in Egypt resulted in the construction of a new city, Antinoopolis, in the desert, while in the empire's opposite corner, his response to unrest on the British frontier was to build the extraordinary structure we refer to today as Hadrian's Wall. His villa at Tivoli qualifies as one of the most wonderful architectural achievements anywhere in the ancient world. His obsession with architecture, coupled with his respect for religion, led to the construction of splendid temples, of which the Pantheon in Rome and the Temple of

Olympian Zeus in Athens are arguably the two most magnificent in the entire Roman world. He even created a 'new religion'; the cult of Antinous, almost entirely as a result of his patronage, became hugely popular throughout much of the empire.

He would, no doubt, have liked to be remembered as a philosopher, but seems to have fallen short when attempting philosophical debate with academics, some of whom he inadvisably sought to humiliate when finding himself academically challenged. While he may have been no great philosopher himself, history will forever credit him with the adoption of Marcus Aurelius, the ultimate 'philosopher-emperor', as his eventual successor.

Two words frequently used to describe Hadrian are 'energetic' and 'curious'. Both are well illustrated by his incessant travelling, as a result of which he spent more than half his reign outside Italy, enabling him to see and experience more of the empire for himself than any other emperor before or since. His tours of the provinces were not simply for pleasure, but resulted in the inspection and strengthening of frontiers, the construction of numerous public buildings (including temples, theatres, libraries, aqueducts and granaries), the conservation of historic monuments, the founding of new cities, and imperial inspections of military garrisons far from Rome in which few other emperors demonstrated such interest. His innate curiosity led to a fascination with religion and the occult; perhaps we see here something of a tortured soul, the most powerful man on earth worshipped by his people but rendered powerless in his personal quest to answer the questions that really mattered to him. His love-life was far from happy; his marriage to Sabina seems to have been a sham, while the one genuinely loving relationship we know him to have had ended in spectacular tragedy. He seems to have had genuine affection, even love, for his horses and hunting dogs, which some have suggested could reflect an inability to find lasting true love with a fellow human being. His love of animals, however, seems not to have extended to wild beasts, which he took great joy in hunting personally, or having exterminated by others in games associated with festivals, such as the 100 lions killed during his birthday celebrations in 119, intended to help raise his popularity soon after his accession. In short, much of what we know about him could lead us to conclude, albeit extraordinarily for the most powerful man in the world, that he was perhaps a rather sad, lonely person for most of his adult life. However, it has to be said that he put his personal misfortune to one side and generally provided sound leadership during his two decades in office.

Today, with the single exception of Augustus, more busts and statues are known of Hadrian than of any other emperor, reflecting his undoubted popularity during his lifetime. His generally favourable press extends back to Cassius Dio, who records that while he was criticised for:

'his great strictness, his curiosity and his meddlesomeness......he balanced and atoned for these defects by his careful oversight, his prudence, his munificence and his skill; furthermore he did not stir up any war, and he terminated those already in progress; and he deprived no-one of money unjustly, while upon many – communities and private citizens, senators and knights – he bestowed large sums. Indeed, he did not even wait to be asked, but acted in absolutely every case according to the individual needs. He subjected the legions to the strictest discipline, so that, though strong, they were neither insubordinate nor insolent; and he aided the allied and subject cities most munificently. He had seen many of them – more in fact than any other emperor – and he assisted practically all of them, giving to some a water supply, to others harbours, food, public works, money and various honours.....'

This account has outlined Hadrian's numerous achievements during his lifetime, but, through his inspired choices regarding those who would succeed him, he was also personally responsible for what we refer to today as the 'Antonine Age' – the half a century or so which, along with his own reign, is traditionally described as the most splendid and peaceful era in the empire's entire history. In practice things were not always as splendid, and certainly not as peaceful, as some historians would have us believe, but nevertheless this was in many ways an exceptional period, especially for those living at the heart of the empire, well away form potential trouble spots on the frontiers. This 'golden age' was only achievable through stable leadership, and it was Hadrian who made it possible; this could legitimately be regarded as the greatest of all his achievements.

In 161, Antoninus was duly succeeded, according to Hadrian's wishes, by Lucius Verus and Marcus Aurelius (Hadrian's 'Verissimus'). In philosophical mode, Marcus Aurelius once wrote, *'Do not be afraid. Everything is in balance with the nature of the Universe. Before long you will be nothing, just like Hadrian and Augustus.'* In one way, Hadrian may now be 'nothing', but, in another, he will survive forever as one of the most famous men ever to have walked the earth. Within the context of his extraordinary life, the Wall along the northern fringe of his great empire, built quite early in his reign, must have seemed to him of relatively little significance. He would no doubt be surprised to learn that his fame in the modern world, due in large part to the history of Britain and her empire centuries after the decline of Rome, owes more to this Wall than to his many other great achievements.

Armed with something of an understanding of the man, we must now turn our attention to his Wall.

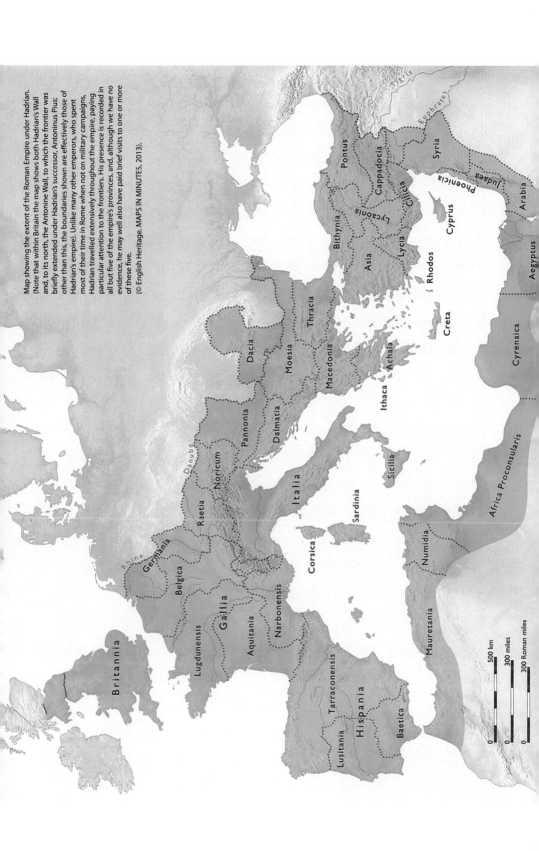

Map showing the extent of the Roman Empire under Hadrian. (Note that within Britain the map shows both Hadrian's Wall and, to its north, the Antonine Wall, to which the frontier was briefly extended under Hadrian's successor, Antoninus Plus; other than this, the boundaries shown are effectively those of Hadrian's empire). Unlike many other emperors, who spent most of their time in Rome when not on military campaigns, Hadrian travelled extensively throughout the empire, paying particular attention to the frontiers. His presence is recorded in all but five of the empire's provinces, and, although we have no evidence, he may well also have paid brief visits to one or more of these five.

(© English Heritage. MAPS IN MINUTES, 2013).

Giant image of Hadrian's Wall at Newcastle Airport, and a replica of a statue of Hadrian in the arrivals area of Antalya airport, Turkey. Long before the advent of modern travel and communications networks, Hadrian was the undisputed ruler of both places and everywhere in between.

Public interest in Hadrian was demonstrated by the high visitor numbers for the magnificent Hadrian exhibition at the British Museum in 2008.

Statue of Trajan, Hadrian's adoptive father and his predecessor as emperor, from Perge, Turkey, now in Antalya Museum.

Bust of Trajan, now in the British Museum.

Dupondius depicting Trajan handing the world to Hadrian. This coin depicts Hadrian's accession as rather more straightforward than it may actually have been.
(© Trustees of the British Museum).

Although issued quite late in his reign, this coin shows Hadrian as a young man, without full beard and moustache. The reverse depicts his adoptive parents, Trajan and Plotina. The symbolism implied by this coin is unclear; it may relate to Hadrian's symbolic 'rebirth' following his participation in the Mysteries of Eleusis in 128.
(© Trustees of the British Museum).

Coins carried Hadrian's image throughout the empire and beyond.

Sestertius from the Tyne at Newcastle showing Hadrian in his imperial barge. (© Great North Museum).

Sestertius depicting Britannia as a seated figure with spear and shield. The earliest known coins to depict Britannia date from Hadrian's reign (© Trustees of the British Museum).

Sestertius depicting Hadrian, on horseback, addressing his troops in Britannia. (© Trustees of the British Museum).

Sestertius showing Hadrian marching, followed by four soldiers. Hadrian had served with distinction in the army, and his healthy relationship with his troops, from senior officers down to the common soldier, was a key aspect of his reign. (© Trustees of the British Museum).

Sestertius showing Hadrian, in military dress, on his horse. We know that Hadrian was very fond of his horses, used during hunting expeditions as well as on military duty.
(© Trustees of the British Museum).

Sestertius showing Hadrian, in front of a temple, addressing citizens in Rome. The temple could be the Temple of the Deified Trajan, one of Hadrian's earliest architectural projects.
(© Trustees of the British Museum).

This bronze head is the only known image of Hadrian (other than coins) from Britain. It was found in the Thames in London and is now in the British Museum.

A similar Bronze head to the British example can be seen it the Louvre, Paris; its provenance is uncertain but it may have come from Egypt.
(Photo: Marie-Lan Nguyen/Wikimedia).

Numerous stone busts and heads of Hadrian are known from all around the empire, including the dozen examples shown here.

Three views of a fine bust in Arqueologico, Seville. (Photos: Caroline Becker; Lena/Wikimedia).

Bust, originally from Tivoli, now in the British Museum (Photo: Marie-Lan Nguyen/ Wikimedia).

Bust in the Museo Nacional del Prado, Madrid.
(Photo: Luis Garcia; Zaqarbal/Wikimedia).

Bust in Napoli Museum.
(Photo: Marie-Lan Nguyen/Wikimedia).

Bust in the Musei Vaticani/Musei Chiaramonti.
(Photo: Francesco Bini; Sailco/Wikimedia).

Bust in the Musei Capitolini, Rome
(Photo: Marie-Lan Nguyen/Wikimedia).

Head carved in green basalt, set on a modern bust; Altes
Museum, Berlin. (Photo: Ophelia2/Wikimedia).

Head in the Archaeological Museum of Piraeus, Athens.
(Photo: Giovanni Dall'Orto/Wikimedia).

Head in the Glyptotech, Munich.
(Photo: Bibi Saint-Pol/Wikimedia).

Colossal marble head, possibly originally part of a huge statue within the entrance vestibule of Hadrian's mausoleum. Now in the Museo Pio-Climentino, the Vatican. (Photo: Marie- Lan Nguyen/ Wikimedia).

Head from Santa Bibiana, Rome, now in the Museo Nazionale Romano/Palazzo Massimo alle Terme. (Photo: Marie-Lan Nguyen/ Wikimedia).

Head from the Dictynaion sanctuary, Crete, now in Chania Museum. This head has been described as showing Hadrian looking weary, late in his life. (Photo: Sarah Murray/ Wikimedia).

Statues of Hadrian, in a range of poses and displaying much variety in quality and condition, survive in museums throughout Europe and further afield.

Hadrian as Pontifex Maximus (Rome's high priest), the most important position in ancient Roman religion, subsumed into the imperial office under Augustus. This unique statue (which closely copies one of Augustus as Pontifex Maximus) is now in the Musei Capitolini, Rome. (Image reproduced by courtesy of the Musei Capitolini).

Statue of Hadrian in the Hermitage, St Petersburg. (Photo: George Shuklin/Wikimedia).

Statue from the magnificent theatre at Vaison-la-Romaine, Provence. Now in Vaison-la-Romaine Archaeological Museum. (Photo: Han borg/Wikimedia).

Statue of Hadrian as Mars, from Carthage, now in the Bardo National Museum, Tunisia. (Photo: Sarah Murray/Wikimedia).

Bronze statue from Adana, Turkey, now in Istanbul Museum. (Photo: Dick Osseman).

Marble statue from Hierapytna, Crete, now in Istanbul Museum. (Photo: Dick Osseman).

Two marble statues from Perge, Turkey, both now in Antalya Museum.

Although many statues of Hadrian are known, spectacular new discoveries like this occur very rarely. This colossal marble head of the emperor was found in 2007 at the city of Sagalassos, south-west Turkey, during the excavation of a great bath-house that he had personally initiated but which was not completed until after his death. The head was part of a gigantic five-metre tall statue that must have appeared very imposing to all who saw it; a leg and foot of marble were also found, but much of the statue was probably of timber, possibly coated with bronze.
(Photos: © The Sagalassos Archaeological Research Project, www.sagalassos.be).

Hadrian was the first Roman emperor to be depicted as a god during his own lifetime. This marble statue, 1.73 metres tall, originally depicted Hadrian as Mars and Sabina as Venus, though for some unknown reason the female figure was later reworked as someone else, and the male figure, although still recognisable as Hadrian, was also partially reworked. Originally from Rome, the statue was purchased by Napoleon and is now in the Louvre, Paris. (Photo: Marie-Lan Nguyen/Wikimedia).

Bust of Sabina, Hadrian's wife, in the National Museum of Rome. (Photo: Marie-Lan Nguyen/Wikimedia).

After Sabina's death in 136, Hadrian oversaw her deification. This much-restored relief (salvaged from the Arch of Portugal in Rome when it was demolished in the seventeenth century) depicts Sabina's apotheosis; she is being borne aloft to the heavens from her funeral pyre, watched by Hadrian. Now in the Musei Capitolini, it may originally have formed part of Sabina's consecration altar.
(Image reproduced by permission of the Musei Capitolini, Rome).

Matidia, Sabina's mother, enjoyed a close relationship with Hadrian, and was an important member of the imperial family. This bust can be seen in the Musei Capitolini, Rome. (Photo: Marie-Lan Nguyen/ Wikimedia).

The scale of the Pantheon's great main door can be appreciated by reference to the tourists in this view.
(Photo: W. Knight/Wikimedia).

The Pantheon is undeniably one of ancient world's most magnificent buildings. It seems probable that Hadrian was personally involved in its design, though we will never know for sure the extent to which the project should actually be considered as his work.

The Pantheon's grand façade. (Photo: Maros Mraz/Wikimedia).

The interior of the Pantheon's great dome, although much restored, appears much as it did in Hadrian's day. (Photo: Matthias Kabel/Wikimedia).

Panoramic view showing the roof within the Pantheon. (Photo: Староста/Wikimedia).

Panoramic view of the Pantheon's vast interior. (Photo: Maros Mraz/Wikimedia).

Hadrian's mausoleum, now the Castel Sant'Angelo, and the Pons Aelius, Rome. (Main photo: Matthias Trischler; AngMoKio/Wikimedia. Floodlit image: Andreas Tille/Wikimedia).

Hadrian's obsession with hunting was celebrated through the construction of a special monument somewhere in Rome; this monument is lost, but a series of eight large circular sculptures or 'tondi' from it were reused within the Arch of Constantine. These show various hunting scenes, including a lion hunt and a boar hunt.
(© Trustees of the British Museum).

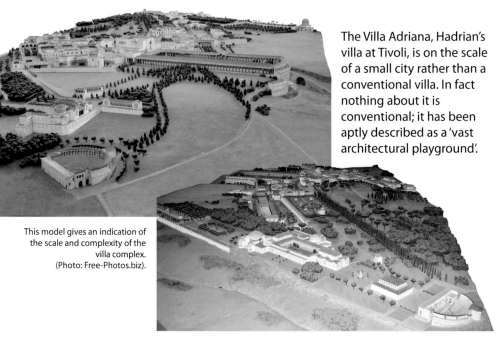

The Villa Adriana, Hadrian's villa at Tivoli, is on the scale of a small city rather than a conventional villa. In fact nothing about it is conventional; it has been aptly described as a 'vast architectural playground'.

This model gives an indication of the scale and complexity of the villa complex.
(Photo: Free-Photos.biz).

Two views of the 'Maritime Theatre', thought by some to have been Hadrian's private quarters within the villa complex.
(Upper photo: DerPaul/Wikimedia. Lower photo: Tango7174/Wikimedia).

A view over the Canopus, sometimes referred to as the 'scenic canal'.
(Photo: Marie-Lan Nguyen/Wikimedia).

Looking southwards along the Canopus towards the domed open-air dining room known as the Serapeum. (Photo: Emiel/Wikimedia).

The Canopus and Serapeum.
(Photo: LPLT/Wikimedia).

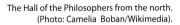
The Hall of the Philosophers from the north.
(Photo: Camelia Boban/Wikimedia).

Part of the huge wall along the north side of the East-West Terrace (the Poecile), looking towards the domed Hall of the Philosophers. (Photo: W. Knight/Wikimedia).

The Hall of the Philosophers from the south-west.
(Photo: Marie-Lan Nguyen/Wikimedia).

View of the Hall of the Philosophers (left) and Heliocaminus Baths, seen from the large east-west terrace (Poecile). In the background are the Monti Tiburtini hills. (Photo: Marie-Lan Nguyen/Wikimedia).

Two views of the 'Cento Camarelle' ('Hundred Rooms'), a huge accommodation block for staff employed at the villa, built partly below ground level.
(Photos: Marie-Lan Nguyen/Wikimedia).

The Villa Adriana's Temple of Venus.
(Photo: Marie-Lan Nguyen/Wikimedia).

Panoramic view of the Heliocaminus Baths.
(Photo: W. Knight/Wikimedia).

Two splendid black and white mosaics, detail of a marble pavement, and the famous Dove Mosaic, from various buildings at the Villa Adriana. These give a flavour of the splendour of the villa complex in its prime, before it was robbed of many of its treasures.
(Photos: Marie-Lan Nguyen/Wikimedia).

The Temple of Olympian Zeus, looking north-westwards towards the Acropolis and Parthenon in the background. The figures to the left give an indication of the scale of this magnificent building. (Photo: Storeye/Wikimedia).

The Temple of Olympian Zeus and, in the foreground, Hadrian's Arch, viewed from the Acropolis. (Photo: W. Knight/Wikimedia).

Hadrian adored Athens, and made some notable contributions to the city's architecture.

Hadrian's Arch.
(Photo: Vikram Bajaj/Wikimedia).

The Temple of Olympian Zeus from the west. The column in the foreground fell in the mid-nineteenth century. (Photo: Chris Fleming/Wikimedia).

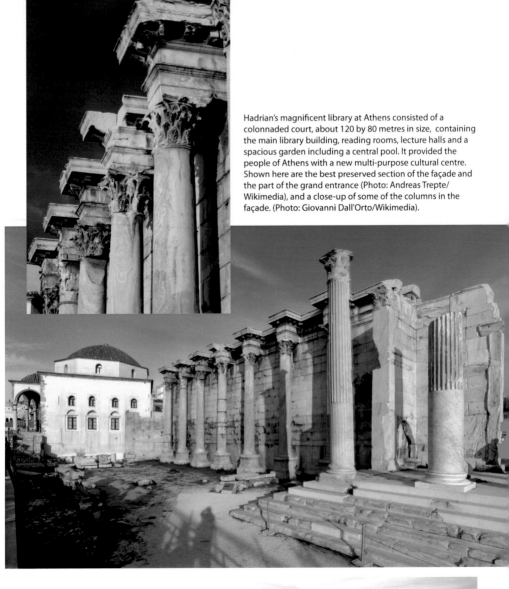

Hadrian's magnificent library at Athens consisted of a colonnaded court, about 120 by 80 metres in size, containing the main library building, reading rooms, lecture halls and a spacious garden including a central pool. It provided the people of Athens with a new multi-purpose cultural centre. Shown here are the best preserved section of the façade and the part of the grand entrance (Photo: Andreas Trepte/Wikimedia), and a close-up of some of the columns in the façade. (Photo: Giovanni Dall'Orto/Wikimedia).

General view of the library interior, now cluttered with architectural fragments of three ruined churches dating from the fifth to the thirteenth centuries. (Photo: Giovanni Dall'Orto/Wikimedia).

In addition to Hadrian's own magnificent building projects, many smaller but high quality structures were erected in his honour throughout the empire. Shown here are four such buildings, all of which relate to imperial visits in 129/130.

The Temple of Hadrian, Ephesus (Turkey). This temple is a highlight for tourists travelling along Curetes Street towards the great Celsus Library, seen here in the background.

Hadrian's Arch, Antalya (Turkey).

Hadrian's Gate, Palmyra (Syria). (Photo: O. Mustafin/Wikimedia).

The recently restored Arch of Hadrian at Gerasa/Jerash (Jordan). (Photo: Diego Delso/Wikimedia).

Antinous as Dionysus, originally from the imperial villa at Praeneste, now in the Museo Pio-Clementino, the Vatican. (Photo: Marie-Lan Nguyen/Wikimedia).

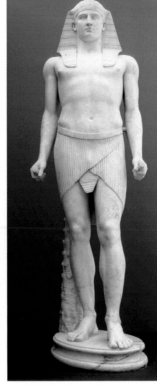

Antinous as Osiris, originally from the Villa Adriana, now in the Museo Gregoriano Egiziano, the Vatican.

Antinous, Hadrian's young lover, drowned in the Nile and was transformed by his emperor into a very popular god. Numerous statues of him were erected around the empire, and his is now one of the most instantly recognisable faces from all of antiquity.

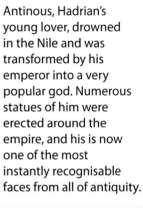

Relief sculpture of Antinous, depicted as Dionysus or Sylvanus, harvesting grapes. Originally from Torre del Padiglione, now in the Museo Nazionale Romano di Palazzo Massimo, Rome. (Photo: Marie-Lan Nguyen/ Wikimedia).

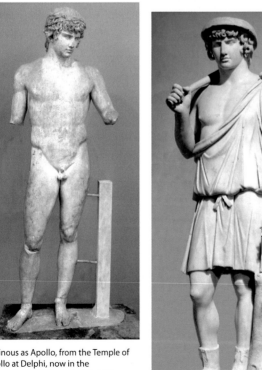

Antinous as Apollo, from the Temple of Apollo at Delphi, now in the Archaeological Museum of Delphi. (Photo: Fingalo/Wikimedia).

Antinous as Aristaeus, god of gardens. Originally from Rome, now in the Louvre. (Photo: Marie-Lan Nguyen/ Wikimedia).

Bust of Antinous from the Villa Adriana, now in the Museo Pio-Clementino, the Vatican. (Photo: Marie-Lan Nguyen/Wikimedia).

Head of Antinous as Dionysus, origin unknown, now in the Louvre. (Photo: Marie-Lan Nguyen/Wikimedia).

Antinous as a priest of the imperial cult, from Cyrene (Libya), now in the Louvre. (Photo: Marie-Lan Nguyen/Wikimedia).

Antinous as Osiris, a restored bust now in the Louvre. (Photo: Marie-Lan Nguyen/Wikimedia).

The Antinous Mondragone, from the Villa Mondragone, Frascati, now in the Louvre. This beautiful head was originally part of a colossal statue of Antinous as Dionysus. (Photo: Marie-Lan Nguyen/Wikimedia).

Following the death of Antinous in the Nile, Hadrian ordered the construction of the new city of Antinoopolis. Shown here are three drawings showing the extensive ruins of Antinoopolis recorded by Edme Francois Jomard in 1798-80: a general view, a grand entrance gate to the city, and remains of the theatre (reproduced from Jomard's *Description de L'Egypte,* published in 1818). Also shown here are two recent photographs of Antinoopolis. The first is a general view over the site; although substantial remains do survive buried within the sands, this view shows how little is now visible compared with 200 years ago. The second is of the village of Shaykh Abada which occupies part of the site of Antinoopolis; the two pillars appear to survive in situ from Hadrianic times. (Photographs: © Clement Kuehn, www.byzantineegypt.org).

Hadrian visited Africa in 128, addressing his troops at Lambaesis where the text of his speeches was inscribed onto the base of a monument erected to commemorate the visit. Lambaesis developed under Hadrian from a relatively insignificant outpost fort to the base of the Third Legion (but note that the headquarters building in this photograph is post-Hadrianic). (Photo: Christof Flügel).

Little is known about the chronology of the African frontier walls, collectively known as the *Fossatum Africae*. This stretch of wall at Bir Oum Ali, Tunisia, could be Hadrianic, but clearly does not bear close comparison with Hadrian's Wall at the opposite side of the empire. (Photos: Christof Flügel).

Hadrian was intrigued by the monuments and traditions of ancient Egypt. His tour of the Nile in 130 was interrupted by the death of Antinous, but he still found time to visit many ancient sites, including the Colossi of Memnon (near the Valley of the Kings at Thebes/Luxor) where an inscription records the presence of the imperial party in November 130. (Photo: Marc Ryckaert/Wikimedia).

Judaean coin, probably struck to commemorate Hadrian's visit to the province in 130, showing Hadrian facing Judaea and three small boys each of whom holds a palm frond, with a lit altar and sacrificial bull at centre. Similar coins were produced to commemorate Hadrian's presence in other provinces throughout the empire. (Photo: Classical Numismatic Group Inc. www.cngcoins.com).

With the possible exception of war in Britain, the Jewish war of 132-135 represent the only large-scale military conflict of Hadrian's reign. This fine bronze head and torso are from the legionary camp of Tel Shalem, Judaea, where they may have formed part of a statue commemorating ultimate victory in the Jewish war. A large commemorative arch seems also to have stood here. (Photo: © The Israel Museum, Jerusalem).

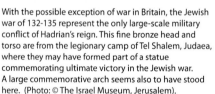

This coin from Aelia Capitolina (Jerusalem) depicts Hadrian as priest-founder ploughing with a team of oxen, with *vexillum* (military banner) behind. It dates from 136, soon after the end of the Jewish war, and symbolises the 'birth' of the new province of Syria-Palaestina, linked to the 'rebirth' of Jerusalem, under Hadrian. (Photo: Classical Numismatic Group Inc. www.cngcoins.com).

Gold aureus showing Hadrian's apotheosis. The deceased emperor is now officially a god; the coin depicts his soul being borne to the heavens on a great eagle. This coin was minted under Hadrian's successor, Antoninus Pius, who oversaw his consecration. (© Trustees of the British Museum).

Antoninus Pius, Hadrian's adoptive son and chosen successor as emperor, reigned from 138-161. Bust in the British Museum.

The Temple of the Deified Hadrian, commissioned by Antoninus Pius, was completed in 145. Its remains are now incorporated within a later building in the Piazza di Pietra, Rome. (Photo: Jensens/Wikimedia).

Lucius Verus, who, according to Hadrian's wishes, reigned jointly with Marcus Aurelius after the death of Antoninus Pius in 161. Bust from Rome, now in the British Museum.

Marcus Aurelius, reigned from 161 (initially jointly with Lucius Verus) through until his death in 180. He was renowned within his lifetime as a philosopher, and remains so to this day. Marble bust from Cyrene, Libya, now in the British Museum.

A magnificent bronze statue of Marcus Aurelius on horseback, now in the Musei Capitolini, Rome. (Photo: Jean-Christophe Benoist/Wikimedia).

Chapter 2

Hadrian's Wall

'And this, then, is the Roman Wall,' he said, scrambling up to a height which commanded the course of that celebrated work of antiquity; 'What a people! whose labours, even at this extremity of their empire, comprehended such space, and were executed upon a scale of such grandeur!'

Sir Walter Scott, *Guy Mannering* (Chapter 22), 1815.

*In few parts of the world are there such evident traces of the march of Roman legions as in Britain. In the northern counties of England especially, the footprints of the Empire are very distinct......
Every other monument in Britain, however, yields in importance to THE ROMAN WALL.*

John Collingwood Bruce, *The Roman Wall* (Chapter 1), 1867 (3rd edition).

Introduction

The complex, multi-phase monument known to us as Hadrian's Wall dates originally from the early 120s. It was not finally abandoned by Rome until the early fifth century. It may therefore be regarded as having been in active service for about a dozen generations. As with our discussion of Hadrian, presented in Chapter 1, our understanding of the Wall is based on the collation of data from a variety of sources, but despite all the available information, and a great deal of speculation over recent centuries, there is still much that we currently do not (and may never) know for sure. Over the years, numerous popular books and complex academic papers in learned journals have been published covering aspects of the Wall's origins, chronology, architecture, functions and eventual demise. In the space available, this chapter cannot hope to provide detailed discussion of individual sites or descriptions of particular excavations; rather, it seeks to provide a historical and architectural overview of the Wall complex throughout the Roman occupation and beyond. Speculation as to its intended functions, and the extent to which it succeeded in meeting these, is reserved for Chapter 3.

This account extends from the arrival of the Romans in the Wall corridor, some half a century before the building of the Wall, through its eventual abandonment by Rome to its rediscovery by antiquarians and subsequent investigation by archaeologists through until the present day. It is presented in five sections:

1. Before the Wall. An introduction to Roman Britain from the conquest by Claudius in AD 43 through to the time of Hadrian.
2. Hadrian's Wall – the original 'grand design'.
3. The 'revised plan'. The great wall forts, the vallum, and the 'narrow wall'.
4. The Wall after Hadrian, examining the history of the frontier from Hadrian's death through until the end of Roman Britain in the early fifth century.
5. The Wall after the Romans, outlining the rediscovery of the Wall by antiquarians and its study through until the present day.

1. Before the Wall

The Roman army, under Julius Caesar, first landed in Britain in the late summer of 55 BC, returning to the continent after just a few weeks. An invasion followed the next summer, when the tribes of southern Britain submitted to Caesar, but again the troops were withdrawn before the year was out. For nearly a hundred years, Rome made no further attempt to annex Britain as successive emperors sought military glory in the east. Then, in AD 43, Claudius, desperate for a military triumph, picked Britain as his target. Within a couple of decades, and apparently with relatively little bloodshed, the south of England was well on the way to becoming 'Romanised'. Previously independent aristocracies retained much of their power, but tribal chiefs were now 'client kings' of Rome within the new province of Britannia, their positions safeguarded, and their reputations enhanced, through association with Rome. Several new towns were built, linked together via the Roman road network which enabled the military to travel rapidly across country when necessary, but which was also important to civilian trade and communications. Despite occasional setbacks, most notably the rebellion of AD 60 led by Boudicca, southern England would pose Rome few problems. The same cannot be said, however, for the north.

Thirty-five years after the Claudian invasion, legionary bases had been constructed in Chester, in preparation for the takeover of North Wales, and York, ready for the move north into Scotland. Northern England was largely occupied by the tribe known to the Romans as the Brigantes. In fact, the Brigantes may have been a loose affiliation of many smaller tribes, between and within which there must have been differing attitudes towards Rome. Initially, under their Queen, Cartimandua, the Brigantes seem to have been on friendly terms with Rome, but by the AD 70s, now ruled by Cartimandua's husband, Venutius, they were vehemently opposed to Roman rule. Before long, however, the Brigantes had succumbed to the might of the Roman military. By AD 78, when the famous Roman general, Gnaeus Julius Agricola, was appointed Governor of Britain, it was time for the Roman army to resume its relentless march north.

Agricola spent his first season in the field, AD 78, consolidating Rome's hold on North Wales, then turned his attention to northern England and Scotland. He moved troops in substantial numbers up to a line from Corbridge to Carlisle, and from here mounted six annual campaigns, reaching deep into Scotland. In AD 83, Roman troops achieved a significant victory over the Caledonians at the Battle of Mons Graupius (the exact location of which is unknown, but must have been somewhere on the fringes of the Scottish Highlands). Mons Graupius was a major battle; literary sources suggest the Caledonian army consisted of some 30,000 men, and the Roman force probably numbered some 20,000. After the battle, work began on the construction of a major new legionary base at Inchtuthil (near Perth), clearly signalling the intention to maintain a permanent presence here. This conquest of the Caledonians should have been the pivotal moment in the Roman annexation of northern Britain. But it was not. Instead, troops were withdrawn to bolster campaigns elsewhere in the empire and much of what is now Scotland was effectively abandoned.

Garrisons were maintained at some forts located on the main roads through southern Scotland, and troops were also garrisoned at forts on the Corbridge-Carlisle road, known to us as the Stanegate. Corbridge (*Corstopitum* or *Coria*) and Carlisle (*Luguvalium*) were very important military bases, where the Stanegate crossed the Tyne and the Eden respectively. Between them, the best known of all the Stanegate forts can be visited at Vindolanda, where extraordinary excavations by generations of the Birley family have uncovered a series of overlying forts, the earliest of which, built in turf and timber, dates from the late first century. The famous Vindolanda writing tablets, miraculously preserved in waterlogged deposits, provide evidence of life in the fort between about AD 90 and 120. They include records of supplies, various official reports and personal letters, including, most famously, the invitation to a birthday party sent by Claudia Severa, presumed to be the wife of the commander of a nearby fort, to Sulpicia Lepidina, the wife of Vindolanda's commanding officer, Flavius Cerialis. Another tablet refers to the enemy:

'The Britons are unprotected by armour. There are very many cavalry. The cavalry do not use swords, nor do the wretched Britons take up fixed positions in order to throw their javelins.'

The word translated here as 'wretched Britons' is 'Brittunculi', a word otherwise unknown; it suggests a degree of frustration at an enemy that was constantly a danger but would not fight pitched battles of the sort favoured by the Roman army. We may envisage bands of natives opposed to Rome (that might be referred to today as 'insurgents') causing trouble at every available opportunity but never coming together as a single army to fight a battle. We should note, in passing, that while the Romans may have regarded them as insurgents, to their own they were undoubtedly freedom fighters and heroes of the highest order.

Trajan became emperor in AD 97 and his military priorities were in the east of the empire; he may have had ambitions to reoccupy northern Britain but this was clearly not a top priority. During his reign, the Stanegate seems to have developed into a frontier; everything to the south was within the empire, while land to the north, for the time being at least, was not. Evidence from forts in southern Scotland suggests that they may all have been abandoned in about AD 105, and that this withdrawal may have been associated with concerted military action by northern tribes, forcing the Romans back to the Stanegate. Under Trajan, a series of forts, fortlets and watch towers was set up on the German frontier, and, while many sites on the Stanegate remain to be accurately dated, it seems that a similar situation may have developed here. In addition to Carlisle, Vindolanda and Corbridge, Stanegate forts probably stood at Brampton, Nether Denton, Carvoran and Newbrough. It is not known whether this 'frontier system' extended further west than Carlisle, linking the forts at Kirkbride and Burgh-by-Sands South, or east of Corbridge, linking forts at South Shields and Wickham. In addition to the forts, several smaller 'fortlets', such as the excavated example at Haltwhistle Burn, also stood along the Stanegate.

There is nothing to suggest that Trajan made a decision to locate the empire's northern frontier permanently along the Stanegate. The concentration of military sites here was apparently a response to a military threat from the north, and it may always have been intended as a temporary state of affairs until the necessary resources could be procured to resume the northern campaigns.

2. Hadrian's Wall – the original 'grand design'

When Hadrian succeeded Trajan, in 117, the situation on the northern frontier seems to have been far from stable, but the nature and magnitude of the threat, and the scale of any conflict, are unknown. It may be that the northern tribes saw the accession of a new emperor as a potential opportunity to oust the hated Romans, forcing them back into southern England or even away from Britain altogether. Hadrian did withdraw from some of the territory won by Trajan in the east, and he may have considered withdrawal from Britain, but on balance, given the degree of Romanisation achieved over the previous eight decades in the south, and no doubt also taking into consideration the mineral wealth of the North Pennines and other areas of England and Wales, withdrawal from Britain was never a viable option. Hadrian, never one to miss an architectural opportunity, responded to the problem of the northern frontier not by despatching his troops to conquer the north of the island, but by commanding them to build a wall across the middle of it. His reasons for this decision, the extent to which he was personally involved in the planning of the Wall, and the extent to which the Wall fulfilled his expectations of it, are all subjects for the next chapter. Here we are concerned primarily with the provision of an architectural and historical overview of the Wall and its associated structures.

The Wall's course does not follow the lower-lying Stanegate, but crosses higher ground to the north, taking in what is generally regarded today as some of the best walking country in Britain. It is debatable whether the Roman troops engaged in the Wall's construction and subsequent management, in all weathers, gained quite as much pleasure from this landscape as the thousands of tourists who now walk the Hadrian's Wall National Trail each year, but we can be sure that those involved in its construction knew they were engaged in the production of something special.

The Wall is best known today for its dramatic central sector, striding across the crags of the Great Whin Sill now incorporated within the Northumberland National Park. To either side of this central zone, remnants can still be seen in many places, though more intensive land use over recent centuries has generally caused more destruction on the lower ground. The Wall is traditionally described, and its features numbered, from east to west. Starting at Wallsend and heading westwards, the line follows gradually ascending ground to Byker Hill, 60 metres above sea level, before dropping into the valley of the Ouseburn, then climbing steadily to the fort at Benwell at a height of 127 metres. From here it undulates, crossing the North Tyne at Chesters before rising steadily to attain a height of 245 metres at the east end of the Whin Sill crags at Coesike, and reaching its highest point, 375 metres, at Winshields. The Wall strides dramatically along the Whin Sill crags, with a substantial sheer drop to the north in many places such as the well known, and much photographed, crags at Sewingshields, Housesteads, Hotbank, Highshield, Peel, Winshields, Cawfields and Walltown. Westwards from the fort of Carvoran, the line descends gradually to cross the Irthing at Willowford Bridge before rising steeply to Harrow's Scar milecastle and on to Birdoswald fort at a height of 150 metres. From here, the Wall follows gradually descending ground (but with sometimes spectacular views to the south, for example in the vicinity of Banks) before crossing the Eden at Stanwix then continuing westwards, along the southern coast of the Solway estuary, to its western terminus at Bowness.

Strung out along this line are the many fascinating sites and features that collectively form the archaeology of the Hadrian's Wall World Heritage Site. It is not possible here to describe these individually in any detail, but we will now consider the main elements of the original Wall scheme: the actual Wall itself, the wall ditch, milecastles, the Portgate on Dere Street, turrets, the defences extending down the Cumbrian coast, and outpost forts to the north of the Wall. Further developments, including the introduction of the great wall forts and the vallum, are considered in the subsequent section. We should note at this point that most of the building work was undertaken by the three legions stationed in Britain, each of which included experienced military surveyors and architects, along with thousands of men trained in military construction work; we will consider the planning and construction of the Wall in a little more detail later.

The Wall

It comes as a surprise to many of today's visitors to learn that in the beginning much of the Wall wasn't really a wall at all. The western sector, 30 miles from Bowness-on-Solway to the west bank of the river Irthing, was originally a 20 feet wide turf bank rather than a stone wall (it was later rebuilt in stone as discussed below). However, it is the stone sector that would have been the surprise to a Roman visitor as the use of blocks of turf, stripped from adjacent grassland, was the normal method of construction employed by the Roman military when building defensive ramparts. Why the Wall was originally built partly of turf and part in stone remains something of a mystery to archaeologists. Some claim that the explanation relates simply to the ready availability of turf in the west, and of stone and lime (for mortar) in the east. Others think the turf sector may have been constructed as the first stage in the project, possibly as a priority in the face of an immediate threat from the Novantae and Selgovae tribes to the north, before a decision was taken to build elsewhere in stone. Alternatively, there may have been simultaneous but separate construction projects to either side of the Irthing; a turf wall to the west managed from Carlisle, and a stone wall to the east managed from Corbridge. Two decades later, turf was used for the Antonine Wall (discussed later in this chapter) demonstrating that it remained an entirely acceptable construction method, and it may be that the decision to build the eastern sector of Hadrian's Wall in stone (and subsequently to rebuild the western sector in stone) was made on grounds other than simple logistics; this possibility is discussed in Chapter 3.

The eastern sector, the 46 miles from the Irthing to Wallsend, was intended from the beginning to be a 10-feet wide stone wall; the so-called 'broad wall'. It had faces of coursed, roughly dressed sandstone blocks, bound together with lime mortar, and a core of mixed earth and stone. It cannot be considered as particularly high quality architecture, but the plan may have been to whitewash it with a lime-based render, thus creating a visually stunning monument.

Both stone and turf sectors are estimated to have been about 15 Roman feet (4.5 metres) high, but their form is not known. A fundamental debate still rages amongst archaeologists as to whether or not the Wall had a walkway. However, the very thickness of the original stone wall, at 10 Roman feet (3 metres) surely suggests that a walkway, accessed via defended stairways within the milecastles and turrets (discussed below), was part of the original plan. Indeed, such a walkway may have been crenellated along both its north and south faces as there would still be plenty of room for a walkway between. The turf wall was certainly wide enough to take a walkway, perhaps with timber crenellation. If a walkway was not intended, then it is hard to see why the stone Wall would have been planned to be so thick; a narrower wall would have functioned just as well as a barrier. It may be that an elevated, crenellated walkway from coast to coast, from which the land to north and south could be monitored, was an essential element of the original 'grand design'.

While the turf wall was apparently completed according to the original plan, we don't know how much of the stone wall was completed to the original 'broad wall' specifications. Broad wall foundations are known in several places, but the plans were revised while construction work was still underway and most of the Wall was eventually completed to a narrower gauge. Some implications of this are considered later in this chapter.

Recent detailed survey by John Poulter provides some fascinating insights into the line of the Wall in relation to the surrounding landscape. Poulter visited every point at which the Wall changes direction and assessed the field of view from these points. The resulting data is complex, but seems to demonstrate that the Wall was originally surveyed in three basic sections: from the east end westwards to Sewingshields; from the west end eastwards to Walltown; and along the crest of the central sector (the direction in which the line was surveyed here is impossible to ascertain as it follows the line of the crags, making many changes of direction, rather than being laid out in straight lengths). This is interesting, but not as interesting as his other major observation, that the line of the Wall seems to have been very carefully chosen to generate the best available views to the south, back to the line of the Stanegate. Views northwards were clearly important, but in some places where a slightly different alignment would have generated much better views to the north, the surveyors ignored such opportunities in order to maintain views southwards to the Stanegate. This is a crucial observation relating to the perceived function of the Wall as originally planned; it will be discussed further in Chapter 3.

The ditch

The apparently defensive nature of the Wall is emphasised by the presence of the wall ditch, recorded intermittently along the entire length of the Wall. It runs parallel to the Wall, separated from its north face by a berm about 6 metres wide (see below). The wall ditch is traditionally depicted as having a uniform profile, some 10 metres across and 3 metres deep (with a channel cut along its base, presumably to aid drainage or cleaning-out), along its entire length, but recent work has demonstrated that it actually displays much variation from place to place, appearing very slight in some places and not to have been dug at all in others. It was clearly unnecessary where the wall passed over the high crags in the central sector, and appears not to have been built in the west where the wall followed the south bank of the Eden and in places along the Solway Coast. Famously, the line of the ditch still lies littered with large blocks at Limestone Corner, where the original builders apparently gave up their attempt to dig through a particularly hard section of bedrock and no-one ever bothered to finish the job. Material dug out of the ditch was placed on its north side, as a counterscarp bank or 'glacis' (a gentle slope leading up to the north lip of the ditch, effectively deepening the ditch while also rendering clearly visible anyone approaching from the north). The variation displayed by the ditch suggests that its form was largely down to the pragmatism of those charged with its construction, rather than rigid adherence to a detailed blueprint provided from on high. Far from being a simple ditch of uniform character throughout, the wall ditch displays many fascinating variations, future studies of which may yet have much to offer our understanding of the entire Wall complex.

The berm

Immediately north of the Wall is the berm, a flat area generally about six metres wide (though only about 2 metres on the original turf wall) between the north face of the Wall and the ditch. In the past this has been paid little attention and was generally thought to be of little significance. However, recent excavations towards the east end of the Wall have demonstrated that it was rather more than just an empty gap between Wall and ditch. In three separate places, excavations on the berm have uncovered arrangements of pits that are interpreted as evidence of 'cippi', clusters of sharpened branches arranged to form an impenetrable barrier, thus forming a third barrier (in addition to the Wall and ditch) to any force advancing from the north. According to Julius Caesar, *cippi* were to impede progress of attackers and render them susceptible to projectiles discharged from the top of a defensive rampart; if this interpretation of the features on the berm is correct it certainly supports the view that a defended walkway, perhaps designed as a fighting platform, ran along the top of the Wall. Close analysis of the berm suggests that it was narrower, and apparently without *cippi*, immediately in front of turrets; exactly why this should be so remains unclear but it may relate in some way to fields of visibility from the top of the turrets.

It seems reasonable to assume that the *cippi* ran along the entire length of the berm, but this can only be determined by further fieldwork. Whether they were part of the original plan or were added later, and the extent to which they were maintained (the timber would require regular replacement), remain matters for future investigation. For now it is fascinating to note that they apparently formed a key element of the Wall complex, but one that escaped recognition by archaeologists until the early 21st century. How many more such secrets does the Wall hold?

Milecastles

Anyone wishing to cross the new barrier would have to pass through a defended gateway set within a small fortlet, no doubt under the watchful gaze of a detachment of soldiers under strict orders to deny access to any potential trouble-makers. These gateways also provided the only means by which troops could pass through the Wall. They are known to us as 'milecastles' as they were provided at regular intervals of one Roman mile (approximately 1.5km) along the entire length of the Wall; those on the turf wall were of turf and timber, while those on the stone wall were of stone. The milecastles display some variation in form reflecting construction by detachments of different legions. They are thought to have had towers above their north and south gateways, and contained barrack blocks along either side of the central road passing between the gateways. Several have been excavated, with finds including coins, pottery, weapons, oil lamps, tools, gaming counters, altars and inscriptions. They were fitted with ovens, indicating that meals were prepared within them for their garrisons. Several courses of a stone stairway can be seen within the milecastle at Poltross Burn; these are thought to have provided access to a walkway around the milecastle ramparts, perhaps linked to a walkway along the top of the Wall.

Recent very detailed survey work suggests that causeways were left across the ditch in front of the milecastles, but that these were dug out at a later phase in the Wall's history as the milecastles became redundant. Alternatively, in some cases, a timber bridge, conceivably even some form of retractable structure, may have spanned the ditch in front of each milecastle. It is not known how many of the milecastles opened onto roads or tracks leading northwards, though it should be possible to check this through a campaign of geophysical survey and small-scale excavation. A few of the milecastles in the Wall's central sector were built directly above crags that made access from the north impossible; these must surely owe their location to a blueprint that specified a milecastle every mile rather than to any desire to provide functional access points through the Wall at convenient locations. Other than the turrets (see below), that may have provided overnight accommodation for half a dozen men, the milecastles provided the only accommodation for troops along the Wall in the original plan. Each could have been garrisoned by perhaps a couple of dozen men, presumably responsible for patrolling the local sector of the Wall. It is generally assumed that these men would be drawn from the garrisons of the Stanegate forts, presumably spending short 'tours of duty' on the Wall before returning to other duties. Recent survey work suggests that the link between the Wall as originally planned and the Stanegate was crucial, with many milecastles and turrets carefully positioned short distances from their 'official' regularly spaced positions to enable sightlines between them and the Stanegate forts. A signalling system between the Wall and the Stanegate forts may therefore have been a key element of the original plan, enabling troops stationed at the milecastles and turrets to stay in constant touch with their colleagues and commanding officers within the forts. Indeed, as noted above, recent work has suggested that the views to the south were perhaps more important than those to the north when finalising the line of the Wall; the same would seem to have been the case with regard to the exact positions of milecastles and turrets.

Finally with regard to the milecastles, it is important to note that many to the east of the Irthing (that is, within the original stone wall rather than the turf wall) may not have been completed prior to the 'fort decision' (see below). Many seem to have had their north walls (presumably incorporating observation towers over their gateways) constructed first, implying that construction of a line of observation towers, a third of a mile apart along the entire length of the Wall, was a key element of the original building phase. Completion of these milecastles occurred after the delay during which the forts were added to the line. So the milecastles were apparently not fully functional until after the forts and vallum were in commission.

The Portgate

In addition to the milecastles, the original plan must have included a gateway north of Corbridge, where Dere Street passed through the Wall. Given the importance of Dere Street, the main overland route from York up into Scotland, we may assume that this gateway, known to us as the Portgate, would have been planned as a very grand structure. It would have been easy to locate a milecastle at this point, but a grand one-off gateway was considered more appropriate; it would come as no surprise if this was designed by Hadrian himself and incorporated appropriate inscriptions set above the gate, visible to all heading north or south along the old highway. The original form of the Portgate is unknown; its substantial foundations have been located but now lie buried beneath a roundabout on the A68. We may assume that a similar grand gateway provided access through the Wall for the main road up the west side of the country, at Stanwix, but no sign of this has yet been located.

Turrets

Two turrets were built at approximately regular intervals between adjacent milecastles; if we assume that the milecastles also had a tower over their northern gates this would give a regular arrangement of towers every third of a Roman mile along the whole of the Wall. We should repeat here the observation made above that the milecastles and turrets were generally built some distance from their theoretical positions one-third of a Roman mile apart, so there was clearly some leeway in the original blueprint with regard to their exact locations. In many places they seem to have been carefully positioned with a clear line of sight back to the line of the Stanegate, an important observation to which we will return in Chapter 3.

The turrets were of stone along both the turf and stone sectors of the Wall, having a single ground floor entrance door in their south faces. At least a couple of turrets pre-date the Wall and were presumably observation towers relating to the Stanegate that were later incorporated within the Wall system, and one tower, in Peel Gap, was added later; most, however, were clearly designed and built as essential elements of the original Wall plan. Those along the stone wall were built in advance of the curtain, and were given short wing walls of broad wall specifications, clearly with the intention that these would be keyed into the broad wall itself as it was built to link the turrets and milecastles. In many cases the wall, when built, was narrow rather than broad, leaving consequently rather untidy wing walls clearly visible to either side of the turrets. Turrets along the turf wall had no such wing walls as the turf wall was built right up to their east and west elevations. The turrets in the turf wall had to be of stone rather than timber, as timber structures would soon have been crushed by the weight of the turf wall to east and west, causing serious subsidence to the Wall and necessitating constant monitoring and maintenance.

Ground plans of the turrets display some variation, perhaps reflecting construction by different gangs, but on the stone wall they generally have internal dimensions of about 3.5 by 5 metres, and on the turf wall about 4.2 by 4.5 metres. The internal north face of stone wall turrets was recessed into the thickness of the curtain wall, the turf wall turrets extended throughout the whole width of the turf barrier. Little is known of the internal organisation of the turrets, although they seem to have had hearths on their ground floors, which presumably meant rather smoky interiors. Stone platforms have been recorded within several turrets and these were probably the bases for timber stairs or ladders providing access to an upper floor. Nowhere do we have evidence of the form of the upper level or roofs of the turrets, but it is generally assumed that they had upper floor entrances leading to a wall walk. The roofs may have been flat with crenellation, or perhaps pitched and tiled.

Bridges

The Romans built several massive stone bridges at key river crossings throughout northern England, one of the most impressive of which may well have been the *Pons Aelius* (Hadrian's Bridge) over the Tyne at Newcastle, though little is known for certain about its form. Although an important structure within the Wall zone, the *Pons Aelius* is not actually part of the Wall which passed some way to its north. There were, however, three places along its length where the Wall did have to cross major rivers; the Eden at Stanwix/Carlisle, the Irthing at Willowford, and the North Tyne at Chesters. In all three cases the Wall was carried over the rivers on substantial stone bridges, each of which was a sizeable construction project in its own right. The bridge over the Eden has so far escaped the attention of archaeologists, but those at Willowford and Chesters have been partially excavated and remains of both are now consolidated and interpreted for visitors. Both saw substantial rebuilding to carry roads in post-Hadrianic times, but seem initially to have been built to the same width as the original broad wall and thus, presumably, were designed to be accessed directly from the walkway which we assume ran along the top of the Wall. In both cases it appears that the bridges were built first, then the Wall was built up to them from each side to incorporate them neatly into its line. The Chesters bridge was carried on a series of elegant four-metre wide arches supported by eight massive hexagonal piers with cutwaters to both upstream and downstream sides. The Willowford bridge had a tower at each end, the one on the east bank linking with the stone wall, while that on the west adjoined the turf wall, though this length of turf wall would soon be rebuilt in stone as explained below.

The Cumbrian coast

Next in this overview of the original Wall plan, we must consider the defences that ran down the Cumbrian coast from the west end of the Wall at Bowness. From the end of the Wall, a system of milefortlets and towers extended at least 40km along the coast as far as Flimby, 3km south of the fort at Maryport (*Alauna*). These are spaced in the same way as the Wall's milecastles and turrets, with a milefortlet every Roman mile and two towers equally spaced in between. There seems to be a break in the system around the Moricambe estuary, which may be because sites have been destroyed though it is possible that they never existed here. It has been claimed that this system extended much further to the south, past St Bees Head and on to the fort at Ravenglass, but there is no clear evidence for this.

The milefortlets vary in form but are broadly comparable with the milecastles of the turf wall, with ramparts of turf and internal buildings of timber. The towers of the Cumbrian coast are of stone and similar to the Wall turrets. In some places it has been claimed that ditches showing up on air photographs are evidence of a linear barrier linking the milefortlets and towers, thus effectively extending the Wall along the coast. The evidence is, however, patchy and inconclusive.

Finds of Hadrianic pottery demonstrate that the milefortlets and towers of the Cumbrian coast are broadly contemporary with the Wall, and they were probably part of the original plan. It has been claimed that the intention may always have been to join them with a turf barrier but that the plan was never completed. A road linking all the sites around the Cumbrian coast has also been claimed, but again the evidence is unclear.

The primary purpose of the Cumbrian defences, whatever their intended final form, was presumably to preclude raiding parties outflanking the Wall. The system may also have played a role in protecting supply lines up and down the west coast, lines that could potentially have been threatened by bands of pirates from Ireland or western Scotland. Despite the effort put into its construction, the system was apparently short-lived as the milefortlets and towers seem to have been abandoned by the end of the second century; most may have been permanently decommissioned when forces were moved north to the Antonine Wall in the mid second century.

Outpost forts

The final element to consider in the original plan is the presence of outpost forts to the north of the Wall. There were two outpost forts on the road leading north from Carlisle and Stanwix, at Netherby and Birrens. Netherby is recorded in the early third century as *'Castra Exploratum'* ('the fort of the scouts'), suggesting that its main function at that time (and presumably also back in Hadrian's time) was as a base for scouts charged with patrolling territory north of the Wall. Some of this territory may have been considered as part of the empire, though extending the Wall around it was not a viable option. Alternatively, it may have been 'enemy territory', occupied by the potentially hostile Novantae and Selgovae, in contrast to the land of the generally pro-Roman Votadini in the east. The outpost forts in the east, along Dere Street north of the Portgate, seem not to have been occupied in Hadrianic times.

Another outpost fort, of unique hexagonal form, stood at Bewcastle, 10km north-west of Birdoswald; this was reached via a road from the north gate of Birdoswald fort. A line of sight between Birdoswald and Bewcastle was provided by two signal stations, at Robin Hood's Butts (Gillalees Beacon) on the line of the road, and Barron's Pike, on high ground east of Bewcastle. The function of Bewcastle, located in wild country to the north of the Wall and well away from any main roads, is unclear; its name, *'Fanum Cocidii'*, means 'the shrine of Cocidius', suggesting the location was of some spiritual significance.

South of the Wall, roads provided links to a network of pre-Hadrianic forts, and to the bases of the Sixth Legion at York and the Twentieth Legion at Chester. The Wall was thus designed to operate not in isolation, but as part of a frontier zone some 200km deep extending from Cheshire and Yorkshire up into southern Scotland.

Summary

This, then, appears to have been the original plan for the Wall; a linear barrier from coast to coast, of stone broad wall in the east, and turf wall in the west, probably surmounted with a continuous crenellated walkway, faced by a substantial ditch, with access across it restricted to milecastles provided at regular intervals, and with additional turrets that presumably acted as lookout posts set at intervals of a third of a mile between the milecastles. The plan was spectacular, but it was never completed as major revisions were introduced while construction was still at a very early stage.

The broad wall seems to have been completed in some places, built only to foundation level in others, and not even started elsewhere. (In the latter two cases, as will be discussed below, the curtain wall was eventually completed to different specifications). In his important contribution to our understanding of the earliest phases of construction, Erik P. Graafstal observes that the original plan seems to have prioritised particular lengths of broad wall, including:

The long stretch between Newcastle and Dere Street (Wall miles 7-22).

The sector to either side of the North Tyne between Chesters and Brunton (in Wall miles 26 and 27).

The sector at Willowford immediately east of the bridge over the Irthing (in Wall miles 47 and 48).

Some short stretches in the wild central sector where natural north-south gaps pierced the crags.

These were therefore the earliest sectors of the curtain wall to be commenced, though not all were completed as broad wall. Elsewhere, several turrets and milecastles seem to have been completed in advance of adjacent stretches of Wall, which would never be built to broad wall specifications. In some cases it seems that just the north walls of milecastles, incorporating towers over the gateways, were constructed during this early phase, implying that the construction of observation towers every third of a mile was a key objective in the original construction phase, with construction of the curtain wall and the completion of the milecastles presumably intended to follow as soon as sufficient manpower became available.

There are sound reasons for believing that the turf wall and the fortlets and turrets of the Cumbrian coast (all of which could have been completed within a single year) were also built early in the sequence. Discussion of the sequence of construction can get complex, and need not concern us unduly here, but it is important to note that, during the initial stages of construction, some sectors of the Wall were prioritised over others; some possible reasons for this will be considered in Chapter 3.

3. The 'revised plan'
The wall forts, the vallum, and the 'narrow wall'

The Wall as apparently originally planned was never completed, a fact usually interpreted by archaeologists as evidence that the initial plans were recognised as fundamentally flawed at an early stage. Whatever the explanation for the change, the revised plan saw work on the Wall itself postponed while twelve large forts were built along its line. It has been suggested that this was a response to warfare on the frontier, perhaps precipitated by the construction of the Wall, but there is no clear evidence for any such conflict during construction work. In addition to the forts, the vallum, a unique earthwork, was built to the south of the Wall. After the construction of the forts, the Wall itself was completed, but to a substantially narrower gauge than the original plan. Four further forts were then added to the line.

The forts

The first twelve wall forts were spaced an average of 12km (half a day's march) apart, although this spacing varied considerably to enable forts to occupy strategic positions, for example adjacent to river crossings. In contrast to the 'original plan', thousands of men would now be garrisoned on the line of the Wall, rather than in forts to the south. These forts, listed according to convention from east to west (with their known or probable Roman names in brackets), are:

Wallsend (*Segedunum*)
Benwell (*Condercum*)
Rudchester (*Vindobala*)
Halton Chesters (*Onnum*)
Chesters (*Cilurnum*)
Housesteads (*Vercovicium*)
Great Chesters (*Aesica*)
Birdoswald (*Banna*)
Castlesteads (*Camboglanna*)
Stanwix (*Uxelodunum*)
Burgh-by-Sands (*Aballava*)
Bowness-on-Solway (*Maia*)

The available evidence suggests that most these forts were completed during Aulus Platorius Nepos' governorship, that is by 126. An inscription from Great Chesters is often cited as evidence that this fort was not completed until 128 or later. The inscription in questions records Hadrian as 'PP' ('*Pater Patriae*' or 'Father of the Country'), a title he officially accepted in 128, but which seems in some cases to have been attributed to him rather earlier. The inscription is of unusual form and we should probably not place too much reliance upon it; Great Chesters may have been completed in 128, slightly earlier, or slightly later.

One fort of slightly later date than the original twelve is Carrawburgh (*Brocolitia*), added to the Wall in the unusually long gap between Chesters and Housesteads. We know this is late in the sequence because it overlies a backfilled section of the vallum ditch, and an inscription from the fort suggests construction in 130-133. Carvoran (*Magna*), between Great Chesters and Birdoswald, was rebuilt on the site of an earlier turf and timber Stanegate fort, apparently towards the end of Hadrian's reign. It is usually considered as a wall fort but actually lies south of the vallum. It guards the junction of the Stanegate and the road known as the Maiden Way which heads south to Whitley Castle (*Epiacum*) in the North Pennines, presumably built to oversee lead and silver mining operations. Chesterholm (*Vindolanda*), another Stanegate fort lying close to the Wall, seems also to have been rebuilt in stone at about the same time as Carvoran.

In the east, the fort at Newcastle (*Pons Aelius*), built just south of the Wall to overlook Hadrian's bridge over the Tyne, is poorly understood but appears to be of late second or early third-century date. South Shields (*Arbeia*) lies well to the east of the eastern terminus of the Wall at Wallsend, but is a key site in the frontier complex, occupying a strategic position overlooking the south side of the Tyne estuary. The stone fort here dates from the 160s, but excavated evidence suggests that a Hadrianic fort stood close by.

In the west, Drumburgh (*Congabata*), the smallest fort on the Wall at just 0.8 hectares, was built against the south face of the Wall between Burgh-by-Sands and Bowness. The date of Drumburgh is not known, but its function seems to have been to guard a ford across the Solway and possibly also a small harbour. On the Cumbrian coast, the line of milefortlets and towers was strengthened through the construction of new forts at Beckfoot (*Bibra*), Maryport (*Alauna*) - possibly on the site of an older fort, and Moresby (*Gabrosentum*), at intervals of about 18km, representing a day's march. North of the Wall, the outpost forts at Netherby, Birrens and Bewcastle remained in commission.

The wall forts must have seemed hugely impressive to local people when first built. They range in size from 0.8 to 2.4 hectares, with the vast exception of Stanwix which covers 3.7 hectares and has been interpreted (though with no clear evidence) as the headquarters for the entire Wall complex. While Stanwix lies towards the west end of the Wall, it is interesting to note that, if the Cumbrian coastal defences are included, it lies close to the centre of the entire complex; this adds some weight to the suggestion that it may have functioned as the frontier system's command centre. All the forts conform to the general Roman fort blueprint, though none are identical. A few (most notably Wallsend and Housesteads) have seen large-scale excavation, while others have seen smaller-scale investigation. Most, however, still lie largely buried within the ground and retain most of their secrets. All are complex sites with their own stories to tell; here we can attempt no more than a very general overview.

The wall forts are of the standard playing-card shape (in plan). On the stone wall, the forts had stone-built ramparts with earthen banks to the rear, while those on the turf wall had ramparts of turf and timber (rebuilt in stone at a later date). Massive towers stood at each corner, linked by a rampart walk, with further towers at intervals around the defences. Access to the forts was through impressive double gateways, one of which was provided in each side, flanked by guard chambers. The towers, gatehouses and rampart walks were presumably crenellated, though we have no clear evidence of this. The forts were surrounded by one or more circuits of defensive banks and ditches, giving them what must have seemed an almost impregnable air. The internal buildings included a headquarters building (*principia*), commander's house (*praetorium*), granaries (*horrea*, for storage of mixed foodstuffs, not just grain), and barrack blocks. Other buildings known from within the forts include hospitals, workshops, storehouses and latrines. Bathhouses were built outside the forts as they would have represented a serious fire hazard within the ramparts. Also outside the forts, civilian settlements (known as 'vici') grew up to serve the garrisons. These included houses, inns, shops, workshops and temples. Most of our evidence from the vici is of post-Hadrianic activity, but it is probable that vici would have grown up around all forts not longer after their foundation.

Uniquely, many of the original twelve forts straddled the Wall, with three double gates opening to the north and a double gate and two single ones to the south. No such arrangement occurs anywhere else in the empire. It is usually interpreted as representing a desire to maximise mobility, enabling troops to enter the land north of the Wall much more rapidly than before, through an equivalent of six milecastle gateways. Not all forts were built in this way; the lie of the land at Housesteads, for example, necessitated it being set out with its northern rampart along the line of the Wall. The forts were built for individual auxiliary units; those towards the centre (Housesteads, Great Chesters and Birdoswald) seem to have been for infantry, while those at Chesters, Stanwix and possibly Benwell were apparently for cavalry, with stables incorporated into their barrack-blocks. The remaining forts seem to have housed mixed units of infantry and cavalry. The garrison of the original twelve forts must have totalled about 8,000 men, probably moved north from forts in Wales, Yorkshire and other parts of northern England that seem to have been abandoned at this time. They certainly were not moved up to the Wall from the Stanegate, as the main Stanegate forts at Corbridge, Vindolanda and Carlisle remained in commission, resulting in significant pairings of forts at Carlisle/Stanwix, Vindolanda/Housesteads and Corbridge/Haltonchesters, though the nature of the relationship between these is not known. The introduction of the wall forts thus represented a major increase in troop numbers along the frontier, while areas to the south seem no longer to have needed as strong a garrison as previously deemed necessary.

The forts are assumed not to have been part of the original 'grand design' because some structures associated with the original plan had to be demolished or modified to accommodate them. For example, Great Chesters fort overlies the site of milecastle 43, and turrets had to be demolished to enable the construction of the forts at Birdoswald (where the backfilled ditch of the original turf wall ditch underlies the fort), Housesteads, Chesters and maybe also Burgh-by-Sands. At Housesteads, the Wall was realigned to tie in with the north wall of the fort, while at Chesters the fort overlay the backfilled wall ditch, its defences at this point requiring especially deep foundations to prevent subsidence. At both Halton Chesters and Rudchester, sections of the Wall had to be demolished, and the wall ditch backfilled, to make way for the forts. Excavations at Chesters have demonstrated that the base of the fort's east gate clearly post-dates a build-up of peat in the original wall ditch, a deposit thought to have taken at least two years to accumulate. This neatly demonstrates that at least a couple of years had passed between the digging of the wall ditch and the construction of the fort. Despite these examples, it is nevertheless possible that the intention was always to add forts to the line, but that their locations were not determined until construction was well underway. The apparent lack of rearward installations east of Corbridge lends support to this idea; with no garrisons such as those of the Stanegate forts to call on, it is not unreasonable to suggest that the intention here may always have been to add a garrison directly to the Wall.

The vallum

In addition to the construction of the great forts, the revised plan for the Wall included the construction of the 'vallum', a massive flat-bottomed (and in places rock-cut) ditch flanked by earthen banks, running in long, straight sections to the south of the Wall. The vallum is unique to Hadrian's Wall; nothing like it is known anywhere else in the empire. In places it runs close to the line of the Wall, while in others it deviates as much as a mile to the south, but it seems to have run all the way from Bowness to Newcastle (it has not been located between Newcastle and Wallsend). Wherever the line of the vallum approaches that of the Wall, it is always the former that diverts to avoid a 'collision', clearly demonstrating that the vallum was laid out after the line of the Wall had been set in stone.

The vallum deviates to pass south of some forts, so its construction clearly post-dates the decision to add the forts to the Wall. Indeed, detailed survey of its line by John Poulter appears to demonstrate conclusively that the vallum was surveyed in stretches extending east and west from each fort (rather than in longer lengths as seems to have been the case with the Wall), thus confirming that its line could only have been set out once the positions of the forts had been determined. As we have seen, epigraphic evidence suggests that Great Chesters fort was constructed in or after 128, and the vallum had an original causeway south of the fort, thus suggesting that this section of the vallum was constructed no earlier than c128. In contrast, the rather later fort at Carrawbrough, dated by an inscription to 130-133, was constructed over the backfilled vallum ditch, proving that the vallum had been constructed (and abandoned) here by 133 at the latest. Therefore, if we accept the accuracy of the Great Chesters date, we may assume with reasonable confidence that the vallum was constructed between 128 and 133; it was certainly in place by 133.

Causeways across the vallum were provided south of the wall forts. The causeway south of Benwell fort has been excavated and found to incorporate a massive stone gateway, and it is fair to assume other such causeways were provided with similarly grand structures, through which all traffic through the Wall complex now had to pass.

In contrast to the Wall, which was clearly planned in relation to the natural terrain along its entire length, the vallum simply strides across country paying no regard to possibly defendable ridges, bogs and other natural features. Its design varies somewhat according to local conditions, but in general the ditch is about 6 metres wide and 3 metres deep with a flat bottom. The north and south banks are set about 9 metres to either side of the ditch. A third (known as the 'marginal mound') forms a lip along the southern edge of the ditch for much of the vallum's length, though this does not appear to have been present everywhere. In the past, it was assumed that the marginal mound was formed of material that had slumped into the ditch, being simply dumped here when the ditch was cleaned out, but recent fieldwork suggests it was a deliberate and primary element of the vallum system; its purpose, however, remains unknown.

Despite the vast amount of effort involved in its construction (Peter Hill estimates its construction to have taken some 370,000 man-days), the vallum's purpose is not known for sure. Some archaeologists think it may have incorporated a road linking the wall forts, but evidence for metalling is patchy and certainly does not support the idea of a road along its entire length; in any case, such a road would not account for the huge vallum ditch. The logical conclusion is that its primary function must have been linked to controlling the movement of people. Whereas access through the Wall in its initial form was possible at 79 milecastles, the revised plan provided access through the vallum only at the forts (the only confirmed exception being the Portgate on Dere Street). Although the milecastles seem to have remained in commission (their gates were not blocked until later) they only now provided access from the north into the cordon between Wall and vallum; passage to the land south of the vallum was only possible via the causeways south of the forts. The vallum's primary function must have been associated with the regulation of movement across the wall corridor, and it may also have served to define the southern edge of a military zone, out of bounds to civilians other than under the direct supervision of the army. The Wall and vallum together may, therefore, have functioned in a broadly analogous way to the Berlin Wall; manned by the military, but concerned primarily with controlling the movement of civilians.

The vallum is often considered as some kind of 'optional extra' within the Wall complex, but it was in itself an enormous undertaking; had the Wall never been built then the vallum would be regarded, in its own right, as an immense achievement. Whatever its function, it clearly mattered to those entrusted with its construction; at Limestone Corner in the Wall's central sector, the wall ditch was not completed due to the unusual hardness of the bedrock, but the vallum to the south was driven straight through identical rock. Given its architectural symmetry and uncertain purpose, it is tempting to see the vallum as part of the architect inspired 'grand design' of an original blueprint, running behind the Wall (with its regular, uninterrupted sequence of turrets and milecastles) from coast to coast. However, the fact that it was not constructed until the implementation of the revised plan has led most archaeologists to interpret it as an afterthought, dating from the time the decision was made to add the wall forts. The detailed chronology and purpose of the vallum remain unresolved and continue to demand further investigation in the attempt to offer a plausible interpretation of the entire Wall complex.

The 'narrow wall'

When work recommenced on the Wall, following the construction of the wall forts, its width was reduced from the original 10 feet to 8 feet or less. In several places, narrow wall was built upon previously constructed broad wall foundations, which had lain dormant for two or three years while construction was focused on the wall forts. This 'narrow wall decision' seems to have been made shortly after the construction of the forts and vallum. Evidence for this comes from Chesters fort; when the Wall foundations were built here abutting the fort's west gate, they partially overlay a backfilled ditch terminal of the fort ramparts, but were still constructed to broad wall specifications. Clearly, the men who laid these foundations, following construction of the fort, were expecting the Wall here to be of broad gauge, although narrow wall was subsequently constructed on the broad wall foundations.

The conventional explanation for the reduction in width is that it speeded up the construction process, but in practice the time saved would have been minimal. The same quantity of worked stone for the wall faces was required (assuming there was no reduction in height) and the only time actually saved related to the reduced need for rubble infill, a matter of little consequence given the effort involved in other aspects of the immense construction project. It is possible that the narrow wall was somewhat lower, and it has been suggested that the revised plan no longer required a continuous wall-top walkway, but no generally accepted explanation for the reduction in width has yet been forthcoming from any source. It is possible that the origins of the narrow wall lay in a decision to crenellate only the north side of a wall-top walkway, rather than both sides, with perhaps a simple low parapet or kerb to the south (a barrier of some kind must surely have been necessary to the south, or walking any distance along the wall-top would have been treacherous in winter, virtually suicidal under severe winter conditions). This would have become feasible once the vallum was in place to the south; the Wall now faced unambiguously to the north, protected to the south by a military zone bounded by the vallum. The removal of a perceived need for crenellation along its south side would have enabled the Wall to be narrower, while still providing adequate width for a walkway along the top of it.

In contrast to the broad wall west of Newcastle, the east end of the wall, between the *Pons Aelius* and Wallsend, is entirely narrow wall, without broad wall foundations, and is keyed into the west gate of Wallsend fort. This, coupled with the fact that the milecastles west of Newcastle are spaced at roughly regular intervals, one Roman mile apart, while those between Newcastle and Wallsend are more irregularly spaced, has led to the suggestion that the Wall's original eastern terminus was adjacent to the *Pons Aelius*, and the decision to extend it to Wallsend came later, possibly as a result of conflict in this area. While this is a fair interpretation of the available evidence, it may be that the intention was always to extend the Wall to Wallsend, but that this section was not started until after the decision to add the forts and reduce the Wall's width. Either way, the Wall's eastern terminus was a short length of narrow wall extending from the south-east angle of Wallsend fort down to the north bank of the Tyne. The original appearance of this is not known; nothing survives here today to suggest that anything of significance stood here to mark the end (or start) of the Wall.

Rebuilding of the turf wall in stone

Another key aspect of the Wall story that remains poorly dated is the rebuilding in stone of the turf wall, extending 31 Roman miles between Bowness in the west and the river Irthing. The replacement stone wall generally follows the exact line of its turf predecessor, with existing turrets (built in stone from the start) incorporated within its line, and turf-built milecastles replaced in stone. Although the evidence is far from certain, the eastern end of the turf wall, between the Irthing and milecastle 54, seems to have been rebuilt in stone towards the end of Hadrian's reign, perhaps in the mid 130s. The new stone wall here was similar in form to the 'narrow wall' to the east.

Between milecastles 49 (Harrow's Scar) and 51 (Wallbowes) the stone wall was built some distance north of the line of the old turf wall, necessitating the construction of new turrets and milecastles. This sector includes the fort of Birdoswald and it is thought that the realignment here may have been principally to provide more land in the vicinity of the fort south of the Wall. The turf wall that abutted the fort south of its east and west gates (leaving three gates opening to the north) was demolished and its ditch backfilled, and the stone wall was aligned on the fort's north-east and north-west angles, leaving only the north gate opening to the north of the Wall. The fact that the new stone wall to the west of Birdoswald was given new turrets and milecastles demonstrates the continuing desire to adhere to the original, regular blueprint, but the realignment of the Wall reflects a degree of flexibility, where local solutions could be developed for particular local circumstances. It is clear that the views southwards to the Stanegate were no longer critical when the replacement stone wall was constructed; this is an important observation that will be considered further in Chapter 3.

West of milecastle 54, the stone wall that replaced the original turf structure is rather different in character and is thought to be later in date, though its detailed chronology remains unknown. It is intermediate in width between the so-called 'broad' and 'narrow' walls further east, so is usually referred to as the 'intermediate wall'. It may date from the mid 160s when the wall was recommissioned following the abandonment of the Antonine Wall (discussed below), but could be as late as the early third century when Septimius Severus undertook much rebuilding work along the length of the Wall.

The north faces of some turf wall turrets can be seen to stand proud of the north face of the replacement stone wall. Clearly, when the turf wall was demolished the replacement stone wall was deliberately aligned to leave these turrets standing slightly proud, whereas elsewhere the north faces of wall and turrets are flush. Excavations have demonstrated that in some places the north face of the new stone wall was set up to a metre back from the north face of the base of the turf wall. This difference in alignment between the north faces of the original turf and replacement stone walls has been reasonably interpreted as evidence of a walkway along the top of the Wall, with the stone wall positioned so that pre-existing entrances to stone turrets still opened directly onto such a walkway, the difference in alignment of the two walls being accounted for by the fact that the north face of the stone wall was vertical, whereas that of the turf wall would have been slightly angled due to the nature of turf wall construction. This is a compelling argument and is arguably the best 'evidence' we have for a walkway along the top of the Wall.

The military way

The military way is a sinuous track or road sandwiched between the Wall and the vallum that links the various forts, milecastles and turrets together. It crosses some very steep inclines in the central sector and was presumably only intended for use on foot or horseback. In places it partly overlies the vallum and is thought to be post-Hadrianic in date, possibly constructed following the withdrawal from the Antonine Wall in the 160s. However, even allowing for the fact that the Wall may have had a walkway along its entire length and that the main east-west road was always the Stanegate, it seems inconceivable that there would not have been some sort of ground-level communications network along the length of the Wall from the start. There must have been an initial network of trackways to facilitate construction work, and this may have evolved into what we now term the military way. Like so much of the Wall complex, the military way remains poorly understood and demands more detailed investigation.

Planning and constructing the Wall

The main elements of the Wall complex (including the Wall itself with its milecastles and turrets, the great forts astride it, the forward ditch to the north and the vallum to the south), all lying within a vast frontier zone encompassing outpost forts to the north, were in place when Hadrian died in the summer of 138. He was presumably kept informed of progress with the construction and modification of his Wall, at the northern edge of his empire, right up to his death, though whether or not he paid it much attention during his final years is not recorded.

Before moving on to consider the post-Hadrianic history of the Wall, we should pause to consider the vast amount of work involved in its planning and construction. The Wall complex represents a huge undertaking, arguably unsurpassed in scale in Britain until the age of the railways seventeen centuries later. During construction the entire Wall corridor must have appeared as a vast building site extending away into the distance. What local people made of it we can only guess.

We know from inscriptions found at various places along the Wall that it was largely built by detachments of the three legions stationed in Britain at the time: *II Augusta* (based at Caerleon, near Newport in South Wales), *VI Victrix* (based at York), and *XX Valeria Victrix* (based at Chester). Hadrian relocated the sixth legion from Germany to York at about the time of his visit to Britain, and he may well have had the construction of the Wall in mind when ordering the legion's redeployment. The previous occupants of the legionary fortress at York had been *Legio IX Hispania*, the legendary 'lost Ninth Legion' that some scholars think may have been annihilated in Scotland some time between 108 (when it was at York) and the arrival of the Sixth Legion. In fact the fate of the Ninth Legion is unknown; it simply disappears from the records after 108. Further inscriptions attest that some construction, and much subsequent maintenance work, was done by the auxiliary units that manned the Wall, but the bulk of the initial construction work was undoubtedly done by the three legions.

We don't know who was responsible for determining the exact line of the Wall, but initial planning was presumably undertaken by a team of surveyors and architects from one or more of the legions. Unlike anyone planning a development of any kind in the Wall corridor today, the Romans did not have to worry about planning permission. However, the construction of the Wall did demand a great deal of advance planning, and there must have been some sort of 'management team' to oversee the huge logistical operation. There may also have been some negotiation with those who occupied land across which the Wall would pass. It is quite possible that compensation of some kind was paid to those who 'owned' this land, but without doubt the Wall was built exactly where the Romans wanted to build it and anyone refusing the terms on offer would certainly have had no right of appeal. The necessary planning would have been completed with military precision, enabling construction to proceed as soon as possible. When construction work eventually got underway, it was organised into lengths of up to 10km, with each legion's work displaying slight differences in construction technique. There may have been as many as 10,000 men allocated to the multitude of tasks necessary to build the Wall, and there would presumably have been healthy competition between the different legionary detachments as work progressed, enabling the entire project to be completed within perhaps as little as five years. During construction, the men presumably lived in tents within the numerous temporary camps (sometimes termed 'marching camps') known from the Wall corridor, though these have seen little archaeological investigation and their chronology remains unclear.

In contrast to the multitude of books written about the Wall by archaeologists with no personal experience in architecture or construction, one of the most fascinating recent books on the subject was written by an experienced stonemason, Peter Hill. He brings years of practical experience working on medieval buildings to his study of the Wall, and presents interesting discussions of various practical matters including: the initial planning of the Wall and subsequent revisions; the quarrying and working of stone (including the various tools used, many of which are all but identical to those we might buy from a DIY store today); the acquisition of other materials, most notably lime, sand and water for the production of lime mortar; construction methods, including scaffolding and hoisting; the probable organisation of work gangs; and the likely methods of transport used to bring the necessary materials to the line of the Wall. After considering all these practical issues and more, some of his conclusions are rather surprising.

Although we are conditioned into thinking of Hadrian's Wall as high quality architecture, Peter Hill thinks otherwise, noting that the curtain wall is of no more than 'adequate quality' and that the specialist masons working on the gateways of forts and milecastles seem to have regarded 'near enough' as 'good enough'. A little more time could have resulted in better training and much higher quality architecture, but clearly this extra time, for whatever reason, was not available. Interestingly, while their chronology is far from proven there appear to be one or two occasions during construction when overall quality control declined dramatically. This can be seen in, for example, differing standards within individual gateways to forts and milecastles, where quality dropped markedly during their construction. Hill observes that 'the philosophy behind the work had changed. Instead of a desire to produce work of good and impressive appearance, albeit lacking in sophistication and careful finish, there seems to have been a strong element of carelessness and 'near enough is good enough' creeping in.' Clearly, this does not equate with Hadrian's usual fastidious approach to his architectural projects, and it is not immediately clear why such a decline in standards should have occurred. However, a possible explanation will be offered in Chapter 3.

4. The Wall after Hadrian

The story of the Wall does not end with the death of Hadrian. Its subsequent history is fundamental to the assessment of its long-term significance offered in Chapter 3. Hence we must now undertake a brief analysis of the Wall, within the context of Roman Britain, from the death of Hadrian through until the end of the Roman occupation in the early fifth century.

It must have seemed to those engaged on its construction that the new Wall would stand forever as a mighty symbol of the power of the empire. However, within months of Hadrian's death, plans were developed for its abandonment. Hadrian's chosen successor, Antoninus Pius, decided to abandon the Wall and advance northwards to a new frontier system across the Forth-Clyde isthmus, thus bringing southern Scotland unambiguously back into the clutches of the empire. This new frontier, known as the Antonine Wall, was begun in about 142, after a military campaign that led Antoninus to adopt the title 'Imperator' ('Conqueror'). Whether the campaign was difficult must be open to much doubt, given that Roman influence over much of southern Scotland was apparently already considerable under Hadrian, but Antoninus was clearly content to revel in the glory of a successful military operation. It may be that the north Britons saw Hadrian's death as an opportunity to cause severe disruption throughout central Britain, although it is equally possible that Antoninus was the aggressor, seeking glory through military conquest and expansion of the frontiers as so many of his predecessors had done before him. His aim, however, seems never to have been to conquer the whole of Britain, but to advance the frontier northwards to the Forth-Clyde isthmus. The Antonine Wall, although of turf rather than stone throughout its entire length, was closely modelled on Hadrian's Wall, with forts and equivalents of milecastles and turrets at regular intervals. The forts on Hadrian's Wall seem to have remained in commission under Antoninus, but the milecastles were apparently decommissioned (their gates were removed) and the vallum was slighted (material from the mounds was shovelled back into the ditch) at regular intervals of about 40 metres, thus enabling easy passage across the Wall corridor, in numerous places.

Antoninus died in 161 and was succeeded, according to Hadrian's wishes, by Marcus Aurelius and Lucius Verus. Just as under Hadrian and Antoninus, unrest in Britain, apparently requiring serious military action, is recorded at the start of the new reign. Despite the huge effort put into its construction, the Antonine Wall was abandoned by the mid 160s and Hadrian's Wall seems to have been fully recommissioned. Exactly why, and by whom, the decision was made to abandon the Antonine Wall, and return to that of Hadrian, is not known; it may have been made prior to Antoninus' death as building work seems to have been underway on Hadrian's Wall by 158. The withdrawal from Scotland may have been related to more pressing military priorities elsewhere in the empire, but the management of the Antonine Wall could potentially have necessitated far fewer troops than Hadrian's, though longer supply lines would have had to be maintained. The details of the Antonine Wall cannot concern us here; the key point to note is that Hadrian's Wall was back in service from the mid 160s.

The recommissioning of Hadrian's Wall, some twenty years after its abandonment, was no simple task. Forts, milecastles and turrets were all repaired, and the bridges across the North Tyne at Chesters, and across the Irthing at Willowford, were widened to take the military way (sandwiched between the Wall and the vallum) that provided a link along the entire complex. The vallum seems not to have been fully recommissioned, though its ditch was apparently recut, and its mounds repaired, in some places. Some turrets seem to have been decommissioned and demolished at this time, but many were retained. It may have been at this time that the fort at Newcastle was added, north of Hadrian's bridge over the Tyne. Also, the remaining turf wall in the west may now have been rebuilt in stone, although the dating of this is unknown and it may not have been undertaken until the reign of Severus (see below). It is possible that the system of fortlets and towers along the Cumbrian coast was not maintained after the return from the Antonine Wall, but the rest of the Wall complex (with the possible exception of some turrets and some stretches of the vallum) was now fully back in service.

There are hints of further conflict in the Wall zone during the reign of Marcus Aurelius, but nothing on any great scale. However, things seem to have become more serious under his son, Commodus, who reigned from 180-192. Cassius Dio's *History of Rome* tells us that:

> *The greatest of the wars of Commodus' reign was fought in Britain. The tribes in the island crossed the wall that separated them from the Roman forts, doing much damage and killing a general and his troops; Commodus in alarm sent Ulpius Marcellus against them, and he ruthlessly defeated the barbarians.*

A coin of 184 commemorates victory over the Britons – presumably the result of the campaign discussed by Dio. The frontier remained on Hadrian's Wall, although influence to the north was maintained through outpost forts; those at Risingham and High Rochester, on Dere Street, may have been founded at this time. The outpost forts, although not actually part of the Wall, were clearly designed to function along with it and must be regarded as part of the frontier complex.

In 192, Commodus was assassinated, leading to a period of civil war within the empire. The governor of Britain, Clodius Albinus, supported by the troops of the province, was a serious contender to become emperor. In 197 he led his army, which may have included many men from garrisons along the Wall, into battle at Lyons in France, where he was soundly defeated by Septimius Severus, who became emperor. Severus' newly installed British Governor, Virius Lupus, found great unrest in the north, and, with inadequate numbers of troops available to address the problem militarily, was forced to negotiate, buying peace 'for a considerable sum of money'. Severus' reign saw a major programme of rebuilding along the Wall, presumably necessary by this time as the original Hadrianic work (which, as we have seen, was not of a particularly high standard) had now been standing for eight decades. Much of the central sector was rebuilt using a hard white mortar that is easily distinguishable from Hadrianic work. It may also have been under Severus that the western 32 miles of Hadrian's Wall were finally rebuilt in stone. (The amount of construction work under Severus led many people, right up to the mid nineteenth century, to believe that he had actually built the Wall, with Hadrian's earlier barrier consisting only of the vallum.)

The peace bought by Lupus seems to have been short-lived. Severus himself came to Britain in 208 to sort the problem of the northern frontier once and for all; despite his major campaign of rebuilding on Hadrian's Wall, his intention now seems to have been to conquer the whole island. He and his elder son, Caracalla, travelled to York from where they personally directed military operations up into Scotland, while his younger son, Geta, was left in charge of southern England, based in London. The massive invading army, possibly 40,000 strong, built several large marching camps as it moved northwards along the line of Dere Street, deep into Scotland, and a new legionary fortress was built at Carpow on the Tay. The northern tribes were duly routed in 209, and a peace treaty agreed. Almost immediately, however, there was a rebellion. Severus, now too ill for another campaign, sent Caracalla to annihilate the enemy. Severus died in York in 211 and his ashes were returned to Rome to be interred within Hadrian's mausoleum. Caracalla, on succeeding his father, agreed a treaty with the northern tribes rather than fight them, and departed from Britain. The legionary base at Carpow, along with many other forts in Scotland, were abandoned. The frontier was back, again, on Hadrian's Wall, where it would remain until the end of Roman Britain in the early fifth century.

The Wall was maintained throughout the third and fourth centuries with no major alterations, though the vallum seems not to have been maintained and several turrets were demolished. Although there are occasional hints of conflict, much of the third century on the northern frontier seems to have been generally peaceful, with extensive civil settlements known as 'vici' growing up outside the forts. In 287, Carausius, the commander of the fleet in the English Channel, assumed control of Britain as an independent concern; following his assassination in 293, this situation continued under his successor, Allectus, until 296, when the emperor, Constantius Chlorus, travelled in person to the province and reclaimed it for the empire, after which repairs were made to the Wall and wall forts. Problems continued on the frontier, however, and Constantius came to Britain again to campaign against the Picts (an amalgamation of previously independent tribal groups) north of the Wall in 306. Constantius died in 306 at York, where his son Constantine (known to history as Constantine the Great) was immediately proclaimed his successor, although it would be 20 years before he would assume full independent control of the entire empire. It is known that Constantine campaigned in Britain, presumably against the Picts, in 314. His son, Constans, was here in 342, also engaged in fighting on the northern frontier. Things seem to have deteriorated further during the 360s, culminating in the great 'barbarian conspiracy' of 367 which 'brought Britain to her knees'. The emperor, Valentinian I, sent Count Theodosius with a large army to restore the peace. Theodosius undertook many repairs to the Wall, ensuring that 'the frontier was protected with sentries and forts', but the frontier was clearly not adequately protected as just a few years later, in 382, another general, Magnus Maximus, had to counter yet another invasion of Scots and Picts. In 383, Magnus Maximus led an army from Britain to the continent in an abortive attempt to become emperor himself; this army may have included some troops from the Wall, but all the wall forts seem to have retained garrisons and these men must have been involved in further frontier conflict recorded in the 390s.

Archaeological investigations on the Wall have uncovered little evidence of the above invasions, presumably because those doing the invading were more concerned with plundering the wealthy settlements of Britannia and disappearing back up north than with destroying the Wall or occupying the province. Where building work on the Wall has been dated to the later fourth century, for example at Birdoswald, Housesteads and South Shields, this seems to have been routine maintenance rather than rebuilding after destruction by enemy forces.

During the first decade of the fifth century, Britain's east coast was increasingly under threat from bands of Angles and Saxons from across the North Sea, and the western Roman Empire was in terminal crisis as many provinces were overrun by 'barbarian hordes'. In 407, Constantine III was acclaimed emperor by the army in Britain. He and much of his army then crossed the Channel, apparently intent on retaking Gaul and other provinces for the empire en route to Rome. It may be that only a minimal garrison was left in place on the Wall. Constantine III may have intended to return and reinforce the Wall once he was firmly established as emperor, but he never was; he and his army were destroyed on the battlefield and no replacement troops were ever sent to the province. In 410 the emperor Honorius, who had many more immediate concerns than the fate of distant Britain (Rome itself fell to the Goths under Alaric in the same year) instructed those in the province 'to look after their own defence'. 288 years after Hadrian's visit to his northern frontier, his great wall was now, at last, defunct. Britain entered the so-called 'Dark Ages', with a range of native British and invading Anglo-Saxon dynasties fighting for supremacy as the once mighty structures of the Roman province, including Hadrian's Wall, fell into ruin.

5. The Wall after the Romans

We don't know how the Wall was being garrisoned when Roman rule came to an end. Troops seem to have occupied some of the forts through until the end, but whether the Wall still functioned as any kind of barrier throughout its entire length, or whether it was being patrolled in any way, is not known. When the pay-chests from Rome ceased to arrive, there was no directive for the remaining frontier troops to move elsewhere and most probably stayed in the Wall area, which they now regarded as their homeland. In the absence of any central control from a Roman governor, and ultimately from Rome, society may have broken down completely, with power being assumed by a number of regional leaders who may have continued to use some of the old wall forts as their bases. As the grand old stone buildings disintegrated, and with the loss of Roman organisational structure and architectural sophistication, it seems that large timber buildings were erected on some of the wall forts. Evidence for this has been found at Birdoswald and South Shields, which seem to have been occupied into the mid-fifth century and perhaps longer, and Carlisle was certainly occupied through into post-Roman times. These places may have functioned as the power bases of local warlords, answerable only to themselves but perhaps claiming authority based on real or fictitious links with the old Roman administration. It is unfortunate that while the building and occupation of the Wall have enjoyed so much attention from archaeologists over recent centuries, its demise and eventual abandonment have received relatively scant attention; much fascinating research remains to be done in this field.

By the mid-sixth century, the Wall was history, but poorly understood history. Gildas, writing in a mid-sixth-century letter entitled 'On the Ruin of Britain', offers a confused explanation of Hadrian's Wall and the Antonine Wall, seemingly having no knowledge of their true origins or histories. Bede, the 'Father of English History' who lived his entire life at the monasteries of Monkwearmouth and Jarrow, offers a description of the Wall that was probably based on personal inspection of its ruins in about 700. He describes it as 8 feet wide and 12 feet high, suggesting that substantial portions of it still stood at this time. The process of its destruction was, however, now well underway. In addition to the natural forces that ate away at the Wall every winter, the Christian Church was now in search of stone for the construction of churches, and it was much easier to remove nicely squared blocks of stone from Roman military sites than to quarry and shape new masonry, even if the stone had to be transported some distance. Masonry from Roman Corbridge was recycled in churches in Corbridge and Hexham, while Bede's own monastery church at Jarrow used stone plundered from the Wall. St Andrews, Heddon-on-the-Wall, and St Michael and All Angels, Warden (at the confluence of the North and South Tynes), are further notable examples. Old Roman military architecture was now being systematically dismantled to serve the needs of the rapidly growing Roman Church.

We may wonder what the masons building these new churches knew of the old wall they were pulling apart, but they were the first of many generations that would benefit from the ready supply of quality building stone. Prior to the Norman Conquest, most dwellings were constructed in timber and it was generally only church buildings that used stone, but after the Conquest there was a huge demand for stone for the construction of castles in addition to churches and monasteries on a larger scale than the earlier Anglo-Saxon examples. Many Roman sites, seven or eight centuries after their abandonment by the Roman military, were plundered for stone, and many portions of the Wall must have been dismantled to fuel this medieval building boom. Medieval structures along the western sector of the frontier that reused Roman masonry include the churches (all dedicated to St Michael) at Bowness-on-Solway, Burgh-by-Sands, and Stanwix, Drumburgh Castle, Lanercost Priory, Trierman Castle, and Thirlwall Castle. On the high ground east of Thirlwall, as far as the North Tyne, the Wall was relatively little disturbed during medieval times (Sewingshields Castle being a notable exception), though we can imagine cart-loads of stone being led away to the south for building projects from time to time. Much of this central sector was used as rough grazing throughout the medieval centuries, and shielings (seasonal shelters used by shepherds who lived with their flocks on the higher ground throughout the summer) were built in several places, taking advantage of easily available Roman stone. These areas were always at risk of raids by bands of Border reivers, one clan of which, the notorious Armstrongs, was based at Housesteads where a substantial bastle house was constructed within the fort, probably in the late sixteenth century. As the line of the Wall descends towards Newcastle, medieval castles (Haughton, Halton and Rudchester), churches and other structures made good use of recycled Roman stone. The ongoing development of the major urban centres at Newcastle and Carlisle throughout medieval times ensured that little sign of the Wall survived above ground in the immediate vicinity of either city; within Newcastle, the medieval 'new castle' was built directly over the Roman fort.

After the union of the English and Scottish crowns, under James I in 1603, conditions eventually became more peaceful in Cumbria and Northumberland, though change was far from immediate in what had for so long been the lawless borderlands. By the eighteenth century, large-scale agricultural improvements were underway and numerous new farms grew up along the line of the Wall, even in the wild central sector. The new farmhouses all took advantage of what was left of the Wall, with Roman stone also used in a range of agricultural buildings and field walls. On the lower ground, to east and west, where stone robbing in many places had already removed all trace of the Wall, or at best reduced it to its foundations, continuous ploughing gradually flattened what was left of the ditch, vallum and other associated earthworks.

Eventually, some eight centuries after Bede, history books from the late sixteenth century begin to mention the Wall. In 1600, William Camden published the fifth edition of his *Britannia*, including an account of the Wall based in part on personal observation (though he was unable to inspect the central sector 'for fear of the rank robbers thereabouts'). Camden offered an explanation of the Wall complex that was flawed but, nevertheless, generally accepted for the next two and a half centuries. John Horsley, a Presbyterian minister and schoolmaster from Morpeth, then produced an extraordinarily insightful and wide-ranging account of Roman Britain, published as *Britannia Romana* in 1732, shortly after his death. Also in the early eighteenth century, the great antiquarian William Stukeley visited the Wall and produced several sketches showing how parts of it survived at the time; the ruined Wall between Newcastle and Byker Hill, for example, is shown as clearly visible within an essentially agricultural landscape.

While interest in the Wall was growing amongst antiquarians, this could not guarantee the sensitive management of its remains. In 1745, at the time of the Jacobite rebellions, Charles Edward Stewart (better known to us as Bonnie Prince Charlie, or the Young Pretender) marched his troops down from Scotland into Cumbria and, due to the lack of a decent road, the English army was unable to travel across from Newcastle to intercept him. As a direct result of this, plans for a new cross-country road between Newcastle and Carlisle were drawn up by General Wade. Wade died in 1748, but his plans were approved by Parliament in 1751 and the road was complete by 1757. For thirty miles, between Newcastle and Sewingshields, the new road was constructed directly on the levelled remnants of what was left of Hadrian's Wall. Had he been around to observe this well-intentioned but unfortunate act of vandalism, we may assume that Hadrian would have approved of the improvements in military efficiency brought about by the new road, but would have been rather less pleased at the lack of respect paid to the remains of his 1,500-year-old Wall. Once the new road was in place, it made the Wall corridor much more accessible, resulting in more new farms and agricultural improvements that demanded more building stone, much of it again recycled from Roman military sites.

Despite the loss of so much of the Wall to General Wade's road, much still survived to engage the curiosity of antiquarians. Further important accounts include those by John Brand (1789) and William Hutton (1802), but that of the Rev. John Hodgson of Jarrow and Heworth (1840) was arguably the most significant. Camden, and all others since, had considered the vallum as Hadrian's frontier, with the Wall having been built by Severus in the early third century. Hodgson recognised, through detailed analysis of inscriptions, that the Wall, though much rebuilt by Severus, was originally Hadrianic, as was the vallum.

The nineteenth century saw the first archaeological excavations on the Wall, by Hodgson and others such as John Clayton, who inherited the Chesters Estate and undertook much work crucial to our understanding of the Wall complex. John Collingwood Bruce arranged the first 'Hadrian's Wall pilgrimage' in 1849, an event that now takes place once a decade, and he published the first edition of *The Roman Wall* in 1850, followed by the

Wallet-Book to the Roman Wall in 1863 (which, as the *Handbook to the Roman Wall*, has recently seen its 14th edition, edited by David Breeze). A detailed survey of the Wall was produced by the great archaeological surveyor Henry Maclauchlan in the 1850s. Much further excavation took place from the 1890s, including excavations at Housesteads fort. The early twentieth century saw fieldwork by many great Wall scholars including J.P. Gibson, F.G. Simpson, I.A. Richmond, R.G. Collingwood and Eric Birley. The information gleaned from such investigations led to the development of more refined theories about the function and chronology of the Wall complex, while also fuelling greater public interest in the region's Roman heritage.

Despite this growing public interest, much of the Wall was still under threat, notably in the rapidly expanding conurbation of Newcastle. In the mid-nineteenth century, a railway viaduct was constructed across the fort at Newcastle, and a third of Benwell fort was destroyed to make way for a new reservoir. Later in the century, the forts at Wallsend and South Shields were largely buried beneath Victorian housing estates. Ruins of the Wall's eastern terminus, between Wallsend fort and the Tyne, still extended down into the river in the early nineteenth century, but were partly dismantled in 1903 when the Swan Hunter shipyard was expanded (thanks to antiquarian interest at the time, the dismantled section was removed and preserved; it has recently been rebuilt close to its original location). At the opposite side of the country, the Wall's western terminus was recorded 'a mile and more within the sea' in 1601, and in 1707 it was still 'very discernible' a quarter of a mile west of Bowness. By the mid-nineteenth century, however, it had gone, partly pillaged for stone, and partly buried beneath the sands (where substantial remains may yet survive for future investigation). The Wall's remote central sector was also under threat. Quarrying had, of course, been essential to the construction of the Wall back in Roman times, but it is doubtful whether any industrial activity on a comparable scale had taken place here since, especially as the opportunity to recycle Roman masonry had reduced the need for medieval quarrying. During the early twentieth century, however, quarrying on an industrial scale threatened to destroy not only the Wall but much of the very ground on which it stood. In the 1920s proposals were developed to quarry 200,000 tons of whinstone annually from the line of the Wall, to be used for road building. This project was to provide 500 local jobs, an important consideration given that Haltwhistle was listed at the time as the fourth most deprived town in Britain. Eventually, after much public pressure, this threat was withdrawn, but quarrying on a huge scale continued at Walltown until 1943 and at Cawfields until 1952. Today, these quarries are classified as 'industrial archaeology', and are managed as dramatic landscape features along the line of the Wall, but, given the development of conservation legislation during the twentieth century, it is most unlikely that the Wall will ever again be threatened by such large-scale destruction. Indeed, the conservation of the Wall landscape is now an international business as Hadrian's Wall was designated a UNESCO World Heritage Site in 1987, becoming part of the trans-national 'Frontiers of the Roman Empire World Heritage Site' in 2005.

During the later twentieth century, further research was undertaken on the Wall by the National Trust, English Heritage, Durham and Newcastle Universities, and Tyne and Wear Museums, amongst others, and many sites within the urban areas of Carlisle and Tyneside have been investigated in advance of development. An important programme of excavation at Birdoswald (1987-1992) was directed by Tony Wilmott for Cumbria County Council, sponsored by British Nuclear Fuels. Ongoing research by the Vindolanda Trust continues to throw new light on the development of Vindolanda, on the Stanegate, not least through the extraordinary collection of writing tablets that provide a new avenue of enquiry into life on the frontier in the years leading up to the construction of the Wall. Aerial photography and landscape survey have given us a new appreciation of the complexity of the Wall landscape in pre-Roman, Roman and post-Roman times, while a number of geophysical surveys have revolutionised our understanding of the buried archaeological landscapes in the vicinity of many of the wall forts. The volume edited by Nick Hodgson for the 2009 Hadrian's Wall pilgrimage, summarising work on the Wall over the previous decade, illustrates the impressive quantity and range of work completed, some in response to threats associated with developments (especially within the urban areas), but much as research-led investigation designed to address specific academic questions.

So much research and interpretation has been done on the Wall over the past three centuries that the study of this work itself, and of changing academic and public attitudes towards it, has become a subject in its own right – what we might term 'the study of the study of the Wall' (as neatly summarised in Alison Ewin's recent book on the Wall's social and cultural history). Given all this fascinating work, by so many dedicated scholars over so much time, it might be expected that we should have a good understanding of the form, chronology and purpose of the Wall. But, as will be clear from the above account, we don't even know what it looked like, and there are still many fundamental issues of which we have no more than a superficial grasp. Why exactly was it built, and how successful was it in achieving its intended objectives? The final chapter of this book addresses these issues, focussing in particular on the relationship between Hadrian and 'his' Wall.

Although some of the detail shown here is open to question, this speculative reconstruction by Ronald Embleton gives an indication of the huge logistical operation necessary to construct the Wall.

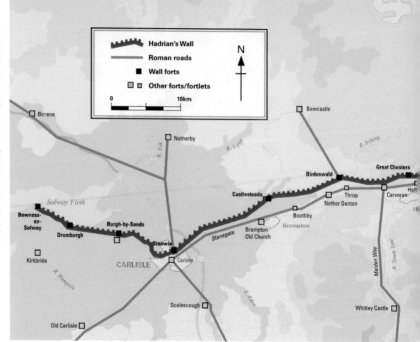

Map of the Hadrian's Wall corridor, showing the general line of the Wall and locations of the wall forts in relation to main Roman roads and other forts (most of which predate the Wall). Note that this map does not show the system of milefortlets and towers that extended at least 40km down the Cumbrian coast from the Wall's west end.
(Map drawn by Ian Scott).

1 The original plan

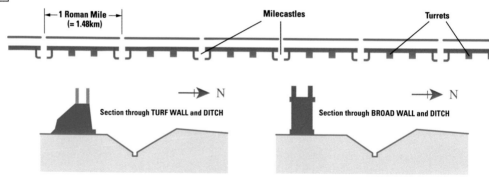

2 The revised plan

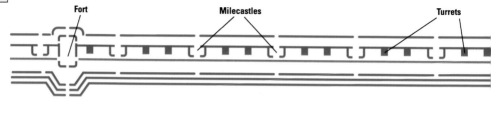

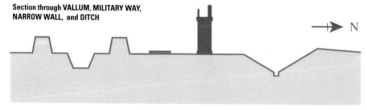

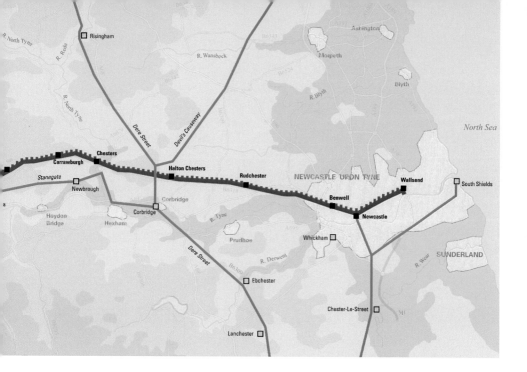

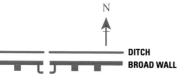

DITCH
BROAD WALL

Simplified, schematic plans and sections (not to scale) of the Wall complex. See text for further details.
(Drawn by Ian Scott, based in part on Breeze & Dobson 2000, figs. 19 & 25).

1. The original plan, on which construction began but was never completed, with broad wall, ditch, and regularly spaced milecastles and turrets. The original plan seems to have been for a turf wall (with timber milecastles and stone turrets) west of the Irthing, with broad stone wall (with stone milecastles and turrets) to the east.

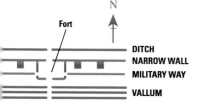

N

Fort

DITCH
NARROW WALL
MILITARY WAY

VALLUM

2. The revised plan, with narrow wall and the addition of forts, vallum and military way. Note that the north mound of the vallum is shown here as having gaps to the south of each milecastle, leading to a possible track along the north side of the vallum ditch that may have linked all forts and milecastles. This may have been an intermittent feature, if indeed it existed at all, and would presumably have become redundant when the military way (the detailed chronology of which remains unclear) was added to the complex. Note also that the positioning of the forts in relation to the Wall is not regular; the two forts shown here are simply by way of example.

Arbeia (South Shields) occupies a strategic location above the south bank of the Tyne, overlooking the mouth of the river. Although the Wall ended 7kms to the west, at Wallsend, *Arbeia* must be regarded as a key element of the Wall complex. The remains that can be seen here today are post-Hadrianic, but there was an earlier fort here in Hadrian's time. Extensive remains are interpreted for visitors, with the reconstructed west gate, seen here from inside the fort, of particular interest – this gives a flavour of the impressive architecture of all the wall forts. (Photo: Graeme Peacock).

Speculative reconstruction of Wallsend (*Segedunum*) from the north. The original form of the end of the Wall, heading from the south-east angle of the fort into the river Tyne, is unknown, but it may have incorporated a monument of some kind.
(Illustration: Peter Dunn © English Heritage).

Visitors to Wallsend can inspect the site from the top of the futuristic tower that forms part of the modern visitor centre.
(Photo: Graeme Peacock).

General view over Wallsend fort from the west.

Reconstruction of bath-house, Wallsend. (Photo: Ian Scott).

A modern reconstruction of a section of narrow wall has been built alongside the surviving ruins of the Wall to the north of Wallsend fort. The modern stakes in the ground mark the location of the recently discovered *cippi*, discussed in Chapter 2. (Photo: Ian Scott).

Immediately west of this reconstruction, a recently excavated length of Wall lies wrapped in plastic, awaiting conservation. The tower of the visitor centre is visible in the background.

Speculative reconstruction by Ronald Embleton of the *Pons Aelius* (Hadrian's Bridge) at Newcastle, with the fort visible on the high ground above the north bank of the Tyne. The inset shows a similar view today: the swing bridge is thought to be on the approximate site of the *Pons Aelius*, while the keep of the medieval castle stands on the site of the Roman fort.

Nothing can be seen today of the fort of Benwell (*Condercum*). Its northern portion (originally north of the Wall) was destroyed by the construction of a reservoir, while the rest lies under a housing estate. Reconstruction by Ronald Embleton.

The vallum crossing at Benwell, originally 55 metres south of the fort's south gate, has been excavated and can be visited, but note that the vallum ditch was originally much deeper than it appears today. The reconstruction by Ronald Embleton shows the vallum crossing from the south-east; the photograph shows the excavated site from a similar angle.

This important dedication slab (1.5 metres wide) from a granary building within Benwell fort, now in the Great North Museum, was discovered in 1937 during rescue excavations in advance of house construction. It records that the granary was built *'For the Emperor Caesar Trajan Hadrian Augustus, under Aulus Platorius Nepos, the emperor's propraetorian legate, by a detachment of the British fleet'.*

Two low stretches of broad wall can be visited at Denton Hall, either side of the A1 in the western outskirts of Newcastle. East of the A1, immediately south of the A186, Denton Hall Turret (Turret 7b) is neatly keyed into the broad wall, unlike many turrets further west which have rather untidy offsets where the Wall was built to narrow wall specifications. West of the A1, and immediately south of the A69, a further stretch of broad wall can be seen.

A long, but low, stretch of broad wall survives at Heddon-on-the-Wall. There are no turrets in this stretch. The circular feature built into the western end of the visible remains here is not Roman, it is a bread oven of medieval date. In this view, looking east, the ditch and berm can be seen to the left of the Wall, and the vallum survives as an earthwork in the background between the fence and the houses.

Speculative reconstruction by Ronald Embleton of the Portgate, where Dere Street (now overlain by the A68) passed through the Wall. Today, the site is occupied by a nondescript roundabout, offering no clue as to the previous significance of the place. (Photo: Ian Scott).

A well preserved section of the Wall can be seen at Planetrees, including a point at which it was reduced in width from ten Roman feet (broad wall) to about six (narrow wall). In this view, looking west, the junction between the two widths is in the middle distance, beyond which the south face of the narrow wall can be seen sitting on broad wall foundations; clearly the foundations had already been constructed, to broad wall specifications, before the decision was made to reduce the width of the Wall. (Photo: Ian Scott).

A fine length of broad wall up to 11 courses high survives at Brunton, including turret 26b. The turret was built with wing-walls to broad wall specifications; that to the west is neatly bonded with the broad wall, while to the east broad wall foundations were laid but the broad wall was never built and the narrow wall can be seen rising up over the lower courses of the wing-wall.

This reconstruction shows what Brunton Turret may have looked like, though alternative reconstructions, for example with just two storeys and a flat, crenellated roof, are equally plausible.
(Illustration: Frank Gardiner. © English Heritage).

Aerial view (by Graeme Peacock) looking westwards over Chesters fort and the east abutment for the bridge over the North Tyne, and a speculative reconstruction of the same site from the south, showing the fort, vicus, bath-house, bridge, and Hadrian's Wall. (Illustration: Alan Sorrell. © English Heritage).

The ruins of the Chesters bridge abutment are post-Hadrianic, but a pier of the original Hadrianic bridge can be seen incorporated into the later structure.

Chesters bath-house, originally Hadrianic but subsequently extended, looking towards the bridge abutment across the river (Photo: Graeme Peacock).

Chesters bath-house, seen from the bridge abutment on the opposite bank of the river.

A well preserved length of narrow wall, berm and ditch can be seen at Black Carts, including turret 29a which has wing-walls built to key into the broad wall that was never built here.
(Photo: Ian Scott).

Black Carts, looking east, including turret 29a. (Photo: Ian Scott).

The ditch is well preserved at Low Teppermore; this view is looking west along the ditch, with the north face of the Wall visible behind.

The extensive views to north and south from the Wall at Low Teppermore can be appreciated from this panoramic view, looking eastwards.

Aerial view (by Graeme Peacock) looking westwards along the B6318 from Limestone Corner, with the vallum and wall ditch clearly visible. The wall ditch at Limestone Corner was never completed and its partially dug line remains blocked with outcrops and huge blocks of stone. The failure to complete the ditch here is usually explained by reference to the exceptional hardness of the rock, but the vallum ditch was cut a little to the south through the same rock, so perhaps an alternative explanation should be sought.

The unfinished wall ditch at Limestone Corner.

View westwards along the line of the vallum at Limestone Corner. The wall ditch can be seen on the north side of the road, above the car. The remains of the Wall lie buried beneath the road.

The milecastle at Sewingshields stands over a sheer drop to the north. This reconstruction shows it without a north gate, but it is possible that it had one originally (as did other milecastles in comparable locations) but that it was omitted when this section of the Wall was rebuilt at some point.
(Illustration: Frank Gardiner. © English Heritage).

The south face of the Wall at Sewingshields Crags.
(Photo: Graeme Peacock).

Ronald Embleton

Housesteads (*Vercovicium*), thanks to its extensive visible remains and superb landscape setting, is one of the most popular forts in the Wall corridor. The aerial view over the fort from the east (by Graeme Peacock) shows the relationship of the fort to the Wall; originally the Wall was planned to run a little to the south of the line of the fort's north wall, as evidenced by the remains of turret 36b, flattened prior to the construction of the fort and now exposed within it. The reconstructions by Ronald Embleton, of the fort from the south-east and the south gateway, give a flavour of the site's grandeur in its heyday.

Towards the right-hand side of the general reconstruction (below) is the Knag Burn Gate, probably added in the fourth century, presumably to reduce the amount of traffic passing through the fort. Other than the forts and milecastles, this is one of only two known gateways through the Wall, the other being the Portgate on Dere Street.

Milecastle 37, west of Housesteads fort, retains parts of the arch of its north gate, though the highest stones have been replaced in recent times. (Photo: Graeme Peacock).

The reconstruction by Ronald Embleton, showing two barrack blocks within the milecastle, is based on excavated evidence.

A small fragment of an inscription identical to those from Milecastle 38 (Hotbank) was found here; presumably there were inscriptions over the gateways here too.
(Drawing reproduced from Bruce 1867).

Aerial view looking westwards over Housesteads fort towards Crag Lough and beyond. (Photo: Airfotos Ltd).

Aerial view covering the same area, looking eastwards over Peel Gap and Peel Crags, past Crag Lough, towards Housesteads fort (just visible near the top of the image). In both views, the line of the Wall and vallum, and the military way running between them, can be clearly seen. (Photo: Airfotos Ltd).

Although located on the Stanegate, and therefore not a wall fort, Vindolanda is a key site in the Wall complex. Ongoing excavations by the Vindolanda Trust make fascinating new discoveries every year, and many finds are on display in the site museum. In this view, looking westwards over Vindolanda, the straight road heading towards the horizon follows the line of the Stanegate. (Photo: Graeme Peacock).

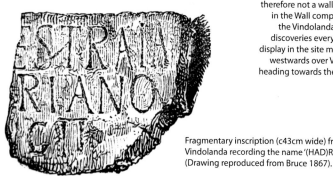

Fragmentary inscription (c43cm wide) from Vindolanda recording the name '(HAD)RIANO'. (Drawing reproduced from Bruce 1867).

Many writing tablets have been excavated at Vindolanda, preserved here due to the anaerobic conditions in which they lay buried. This one includes an appeal by an unknown man to 'Your Majesty', and thus may relate to Hadrian's visit in 122. (© The Vindolanda Trust).

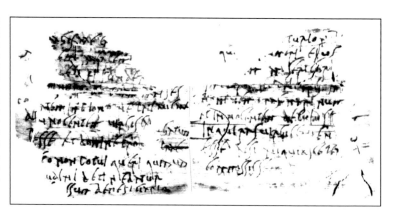

Full scale reconstructions of short stretches of the stone wall and turf wall can be seen at Vindolanda. (© The Vindolanda Trust).

Looking east along the Wall towards Cuddy's Crags and Housesteads. (Photo: Graeme Peacock).

Two inscriptions from Hotbank Milecastle (milecastle 38) recording that the structure was built by the Second Legion for Hadrian and Nepos (the British Governor). Inscriptions like this are though to have stood above the north and south gates of all the milecastles. (Drawings reproduced from Bruce 1867).

A winter view westwards along the line of the Wall and Crag Lough from Hotbank Crags. (Photo: Graeme Peacock).

The Wall at Sycamore Gap, a popular location for visitors following its use in the Kevin Costner film *Robin Hood Prince of Thieves*. (Photo: Graeme Peacock).

The dramatic view westwards along the Wall over Sycamore Gap towards Steel Rigg. (Photo: Graeme Peacock).

View eastwards over Castle Nick Milecastle (milecastle 39), built in a hollow but still with a steep drop to the north, meaning this could never have been a busy route through the Wall.
(Photo: Graeme Peacock).

Peel Gap Tower was added some time after the initial construction of the Wall. It was built onto the south side of the Wall, presumably because it was recognised that an extra tower was needed to guard a potential weak point here, midway between turrets 39a and 39b.
(Photo: Graeme Peacock).

This panoramic view shows the Wall striding over Peel Crags; Peel Gap Turret lies in the dip to the right.

A classic view of the Wall, Crag Lough from Steel Rigg. (Photo: Graeme Peacock).

Winshields Crags, looking east.
(Photo: Graeme Peacock).

The highest point on the line of the Wall – the OS trig point on Winshields Crags at 375 metres above sea level. Note the erosion around the base of the trig point, resulting from the combined effects of visitor pressure and the Northumbrian weather.

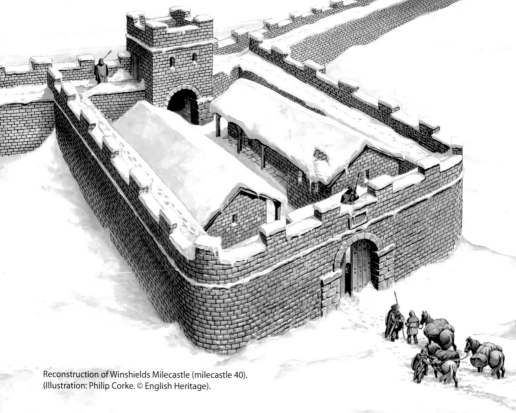

Reconstruction of Winshields Milecastle (milecastle 40).
(Illustration: Philip Corke. © English Heritage).

The remains of Caw Gap Turret (turret 41a) show clear evidence of demolition; at some point the turret was deemed surplus to requirements and demolished, though its footprint remains, just one or two courses high. The recess in the Wall was infilled so the Wall passed neatly over the site without interruption.

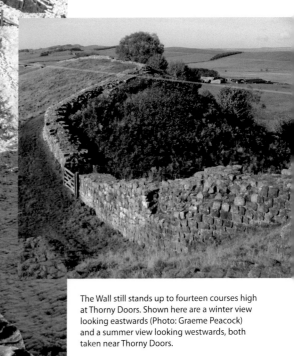

The Wall still stands up to fourteen courses high at Thorny Doors. Shown here are a winter view looking eastwards (Photo: Graeme Peacock) and a summer view looking westwards, both taken near Thorny Doors.

The milecastle at Cawfields (milecastle 42) is dramatically sited on a steep south-facing slope. Its north wall is of broad wall gauge, while its other walls, and the Wall to east and west, are of narrow gauge and not bonded into the north wall. This suggests the north wall, with gateway and tower, was built first, with the rest added perhaps a couple of years later. (Photo: Graeme Peacock).

A small part of an inscription was found here, suggesting that inscriptions like those from Hotbank (milecastle 38) were also set above the milecastle entrances here. (Drawing reproduced from Bruce 1867).

This reconstruction shows the internal buildings stepped down in response to the natural slope of the land. (Illustration: Philip Corke. © English Heritage).

A classic aerial view looking eastwards over Cawfields Quarry and Cawfields Milecastle. Clearly visible are the Wall running along the crest of Cawfield Crags, and the vallum running dead straight towards Shield on the Wall Farm, after which it turns slightly to the south towards Winshields Farm in the trees at the top-right corner. (Photo: Airfotos Ltd).

Aesica (Great Chesters) has a unique atmosphere, contrasting with the manicured and neatly interpreted interior of Housesteads and making it a favourite site of many who walk the Wall. It is interesting for many reasons, not least the aqueduct that brought fresh water to the fort from 10km to the north, and the hoard of exquisite Roman gold and silver jewellery found here in 1894. The fort's internal buildings are largely buried, but fascinating features which can be seen include the vaulted strongroom within the headquarters building, the west and south gateways, and the north-west and south-west corner towers. This aerial view shows the fort from the north; the remains of the Wall can be seen abutting the fort's north-west corner, and the four banks and ditches of the fort's western ramparts are also clearly visible. The modern farm complex encroaches upon the fort in the north-east. (Photo: Ian Bracegirdle).

This inscription from Great Chesters, now in Chesters Museum, was found outside the fort's east gate. It includes the letters 'PP', referring to the title Pater Patriae ('Father of the Country') which Hadrian only accepted in 128, suggesting that the fort (or at least this part of it) dates from after this time. However, this would render the fort surprisingly late in the building sequence, and its chronology remains in doubt. (Drawing reproduced from Bruce 1867).

This view eastwards over the fort's south gateway shows an altar standing amidst the ruins, and, in the distance, the high crags over which the Wall passes. (Photo: Stan Beckensall).

General view looking west over the Wall at Walltown. (Photo: Ian Scott).

Walltown Crags Turret (turret 45a) was originally a free-standing observation tower, later incorporated into the Wall. (Photo: Ian Scott). The aerial view (by Graeme Peacock) looks westwards over the turret, while the reconstruction (by Ronald Embleton) looks eastwards with the turret in the middle distance and milecastle 45 (Walltown) behind.

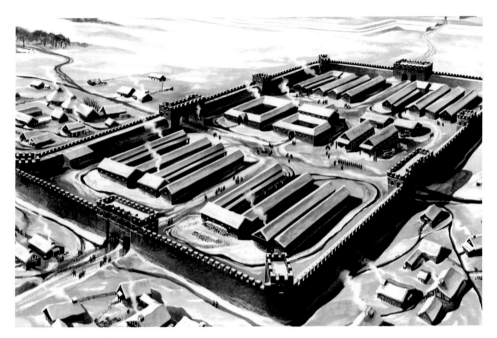

This inscription, recording building work by the Twentieth Legion under Hadrian, comes from Chapel House Milecastle (milecastle 47), 2km west of Carvoran. (Drawing reproduced from Bruce 1867).

Reconstruction looking north-westwards over Carvoran (*Magna*) fort, by Ronald Embleton. This fort occupies a strategic location at the junction of the Stanegate and the Maiden Way. It lies 250 metres south of the Wall, which it predates, and thus should not be considered a true 'wall fort'. The vallum (visible here in the background) passes to the north of the fort and deviates to avoid a substantial area between it and the fort's north gate; something of significance presumably occupied this area at the time of the vallum's construction. The site was ravaged by agricultural 'improvement' during the seventeenth and eighteenth centuries, and today there is little to see on the ground, although the Roman Army Museum here is well worth a visit.

Thirlwall Castle was built in the fourteenth century just north of the line of the Wall, less than a kilometre north-west of Carvoran. It was built almost entirely of 'recycled' Roman stone, thus accounting for the poor survival of the Wall in this area. (Photo: Graeme Peacock).

A general view over Poltross Burn Milecastle (milecastle 48).
The Newcastle and Carlisle Railway, built in the 1830s, crosses the
line of the Wall adjacent to the milecastle's north-west corner.

The Wall approaching the eastern wing-wall of the
milecastle, showing the horizontal offset where the
narrow wall was built on broad wall foundations, and the
vertical offset where the narrow wall meets the
milecastle's broad wing-wall.

The remains of barrack blocks within the milecastle.

The internal staircase at Poltross Burn presumably lead to a walkway around the top of the milecastle walls, perhaps linked to a walkway along the top of the Wall. The angle of the stairs suggests the milecastle walls were at least 4.6 metres (15 feet high), but they may have been appreciably higher.

A fascinating stretch of Wall, including two turrets, can be inspected at Willowford. In these views of the Wall's south face, broad wall foundations can be seen underlying the narrow wall. There are various reasons for believing that Willowford may have seen some of the earliest construction work on the line of the stone wall, even though little of the Wall here seems to have been completed to the original broad gauge specifications.

Two views along the wall ditch, the base of which is followed by the present-day track, near Willowford Farm. The berm and north face of the Wall are visible in both images.

Turret 48a (Willowford East) from the east, clearly showing the junction between the turret's broad wing-wall and the narrow wall.

Turret 48b (Willowford West) from the east, showing the turret's broad wing-wall and, in the foreground, broad wall foundations extending from beneath the south face of the narrow wall.

This reconstruction (by Ronald Embleton) shows Harrow's Scar Milecastle (milecastle 49) and Willowford Bridge. Today, the remains of the milecastle can be visited, and from the line of the Wall here the east abutment of the bridge can be seen on the opposite side of the river Irthing. (Photo, opposite, by Graeme Peacock). The remains of the bridge abutment are complex and result from more than one phase.

Looking east along the line of the Wall between Birdoswald fort and milecastle 49. The high crags over which the Wall runs can be seen in the distance. (Photo: Graeme Peacock).

The view out through the east gate of Birdoswald fort, with the south face of the Wall visible in the middle distance, heading directly towards the high crags on the far horizon.

Reconstruction of Birdoswald fort from the north-west. (Illustration: Philip Corke. © English Heritage).

The Wall approaching the north-west corner of the fort, as seen in the foreground of the above reconstruction. The section of Wall that directly abutted the fort's north-west angle has been dismantled to create a gap for a road into Birdoswald Farm, the buildings of which occupy the north-west corner of the fort interior.

The Wall immediately west of Birdoswald. The replacement stone wall here was built some distance to the north of the dismantled turf wall, meaning that new turrets had to be provided. (Photo: Graeme Peacock).

Turret 49b, looking east towards Birdoswald fort (in the trees in the background) was built at the same time as the replacement stone wall. Consequently it does not protrude beyond the stone wall's north face, in contrast to other turf wall turrets such as 51a and 51b.

Reconstruction of turf wall milecastle 50 (High House) by Ronald Embleton. Due to the realignment of the wall west of Birdoswald, this sector of the turf wall was not directly built over in stone, making this the only turf wall milecastle not to have been rebuilt in stone. The line of the turf wall and its ditch survive as earthworks west of Birdoswald as far as milecastle 51. High House Milecastle has been excavated, demonstrating that its gates and other structures were dismantled in an orderly manner when the site was abandoned in favour of the new stone milecastle to the north. The excavations uncovered a small fragment of a wooden inscription that has been interpreted as part of a panel naming both Hadrian and Nepos, apparently a timber version of the inscriptions that stood above the entrances of the stone milecastles.

The turrets at Piper Syke (51a), left, and Leahill (51b), below, were originally built for the turf wall; their north faces stand slightly proud of the Wall's north face, and they are not bonded into the Wall.

Pike Hill signal tower was originally built as a standalone observation or signal tower, linked to the forts at Nether Denton and Boothby to the south on the Stanegate. When the Wall was built, its line was tweaked to incorporate the tower, which stands at an awkward angle in relation to the Wall. Sadly much of the tower was demolished during nineteenth-century road construction, but the entrance survives, through which extensive views to the south can still be appreciated.

Turret 52a (Banks East) was originally part of the turf wall; its north face protrudes slightly from that of the replacement stone wall. The extensive views to the south here are very impressive.
(Reconstruction: Philip Corke. © English Heritage).

A short but impressive stretch of Wall, largely rebuilt in the nineteenth century, can be seen at Harehill, north of Lanercost Priory. This is the westernmost fragment of the Wall that can still be seen standing; from here to its western terminus it was extensively exploited for building stone during medieval and post-medieval times so that today there is nothing left above ground.
(Photo: Graeme Peacock).

Much of the Wall was 'recycled' to provide building stone for Lanercost Priory, founded in 1169 and now itself a key visitor attraction on the line of the Wall.

Stanwix (*Uxelodunum*) was the largest of all the Wall forts, home to the most prestigious unit of the Wall garrison and perhaps to the overall Wall commander, if such a position ever existed. Today, nothing is visible of the fort or the Wall here; all that can be seen is an information panel in the Cumbria Park Hotel car park, within which the line of the fort's north Wall is laid out with bricks set into the tarmac. Much Roman masonry will have been recycled within later buildings here, but extensive remains of the fort, together with its vicus and cemetery, must still lie buried; sadly, future opportunities to examine these will probably be few and far between.

Although there is relatively little to see of the west end of the Wall, three remarkable finds, dating probably from the mid second century, record the names of forts here. These bronze 'pans' (*paterae* or *trullae*) were probably made in a workshop somewhere close to the Wall, and may have been souvenirs purchased by visitors or serving soldiers. The Staffordshire Moorlands Pan (left) incorporates beautiful abstract artwork that recalls native Celtic artistic tradition. It also includes the words 'VALI AELI', suggesting that the Roman name for the Wall may have been 'VALLUM AELII' or 'the Wall of Hadrian'. The Rudge Cup (below left) and Amiens Skillet (below right) appear to depict stylised representations of the Wall. (Photos © Tullie House Museum and Art Gallery Trust).

The west end of the Wall seems to have entered the south side of the Solway estuary at Bowness-on-Solway, much as its east end entered the north side of the Tyne at Wallsend. A monument marking the Wall's west end may have stood here and it is conceivable that remains of it could lie buried within the sands, though no trace is currently visible either on land or beneath the waves. (Photo: Graeme Peacock).

Beyond Bowness, a system of milefortlets and towers extended at least 40km down the Cumbrian coast. This coast was also defended by half a dozen forts extending as far south as Ravenglass. This fine inscription, recording construction work by the 20th Legion during Hadrian's reign, is from the fort at Moresby, some 60km down the coast from Bowness. (Drawing reproduced from Bruce 1867).

Although we have no firm evidence for them, grand monuments may originally have stood at each end of the Wall corridor. This reconstruction, by Ronald Embleton, shows what such a monument at the east end, overlooking the Tyne estuary and the North Sea, may have looked like.

When contemplating the Wall and its impact on contemporary communities, it is worth recalling that at the time the Romans arrived in northern England few local people had experienced architecture on a scale any greater than settlements like this. (Reconstruction, based on an excavated example north of the Wall, by Ronald Embleton).

Today, the story of the Wall is brought vividly to life at several museums, most notably the Great North Museum in Newcastle (top; photos © Great North Museum), Tullie House in Carlisle (centre; photos © Tullie House Museum and Art Gallery Trust), and the Roman Army Museum at Carvoran (bottom; photos © The Vindolanda Trust).

Occasional special events serve to demonstrate and enhance public enthusiasm for the Wall, reflecting its importance to modern communities. Shown here is *'Lighting the Wall'* in March 2010, when 500 volunteers lit beacons along the entire line of the Wall to commemorate the 1600th anniversary of the end of Roman Britain. (Photo: Stuart Herbert).

Something of the Wall's influence over contemporary life can be seen in the naming of numerous places and institutions. Shown here are a school adjacent to *Arbeia* fort (South Shields), a cycleway near *Segedunum* fort (Wallsend), the village of Wall (near Hexham) with its splendid Hadrian Hotel, a footbridge on the campus of Newcastle University, an industrial estate at Haltwhistle, and a vets in Hexham. Also shown is the logo of the recently disbanded Tynedale Council.

Chapter 3

Hadrian and his Wall

Hadrian set out for Britain where he reformed many things, and, the first to do so, erected a wall over a length of 80 miles to force apart the Romans and barbarians.

Historia Augusta (late 4th century AD).

Hadrian's Wall is the concept of Hadrian much more than the Stanegate system is of Trajan; it is an accurate reflection of the man and his policies.

David Breeze and Brian Dobson, 2000.

Introduction

Chapter 1 of this book presents what we know of Hadrian the man. Chapter 2 summarises our current knowledge of the Wall. This final chapter discusses the relationship between Hadrian and his Wall. It does so by attempting to answer three separate, but interrelated, questions:

1. To what extent was Hadrian personally involved in the design of 'his' Wall?
2. Why was Hadrian's Wall built?
3. How successful was the Wall in meeting its intended objectives, both during Hadrian's lifetime and subsequently?

A brief summary, *Hadrian's Wall – Alternative Interpretations*, then brings the book to a close.

1. To what extent was Hadrian personally involved in the design of 'his' Wall?

Back in the mid-nineteenth century, the great Wall scholar, John Collingwood Bruce, wrote:

The supposition that Hadrian built the Wall is consistent with the accounts which historians give us of his attachment to architectural undertakings. He was eminently a great builder; numerous works of magnitude and merit in the most distant parts of his great empire bear witness to the fact even at this hour. The castle of St. Angelo, at Rome, may be taken as an example. Though intended by him simply for the repose of his remains, and though, as we now see it, it has been shorn of its original proportions, it has formed for centuries the principal fortress of Rome. We may safely conclude that Hadrian was the builder of the Wall.

Ever since these thoughts were published, there has been a general assumption that Hadrian was the architect of 'his' Wall, but what is the evidence for his direct involvement in the project? The short answer is very little. There is no doubt that the Wall was originally built in the 120s, during Hadrian's reign, nor that Hadrian came to Britain in the year 122. But we don't know whether the Wall was begun prior to, during, or after the imperial visit. Nor do we know whether the emperor actually visited the frontier zone; he presumably visited London, and perhaps York, but may have been in the province for just a few weeks, allowing little, if any, time for detailed inspection of the frontier. In seeking to resolve this issue, there is, of course, a further complication relating to the 'revised plan'. If Hadrian did design the Wall, was it the initial plan, or the revised plan with the forts and vallum, for which he was responsible?

Hadrian could simply have authorised, from a distance, the construction of a barrier along the frontier, leaving the details of design and construction to the provincial governor and his staff. This would have been a quite normal level of involvement for an emperor; the key strategic decision was his, but the project planning necessary for such a vast project, and the management of the construction work, was left to the provincial governor and the military. Other emperors may have worked this way, but Hadrian was different, and I suspect his involvement in the design of the Wall was rather more hands on.

We know, from evidence discussed in Chapter 1, that Hadrian fancied himself as an architect, but also that his reputation as a military man was very important to him. It mattered greatly to him that he was respected by the troops, not just to the extent that any emperor relied upon the support of the army, but also because he liked to think that the soldiers regarded their emperor as 'one of their own'. In turning his back on further military expansion, Hadrian must have faced opposition from senior army officers. The army had evolved into the world's most efficient fighting force as the empire expanded, yet here was an emperor, himself an experienced and decorated soldier, who seemed to be saying that enough was enough; the emphasis would now be on consolidation rather than further expansion. What would be the role of the troops in this new world? Hadrian cared very much about the welfare of the men on the ground, and such matters must have been at the forefront of his mind during his inspection of Britannia.

We are told by Hadrian's biographer that 'the Britons were not able to be restrained under Roman control' at the start of his reign, but we don't know whether the problems in Britain primarily involved native communities within the province, incursions by tribal groups from the north, or a combination of the two. It is usually assumed, however, that the frontier along the Stanegate was under threat from the north. Traditionally, the response would have been a punitive military campaign north of the frontier to nullify the threat, if not actually to annexe the territory of the enemy. Hadrian may have authorised a campaign in the north, but his frontier policy meant there would be no attempt to extend the empire in this direction. Pacifying the situation on the frontier presumably took at least a year, perhaps two, and may well have been a messy operation; rather than a set battle as favoured by the Roman army, it presumably involved what we would refer to today as guerrilla warfare on the part of the Britons. Whether the Britons wished to see the overthrow of Roman rule in the region, or were more intent on plunder, cannot be known. Hadrian may also have sought peace on the frontier through negotiation; a promise on the part of Rome not to invade land north of the frontier zone may have led to compromise on the part of native rulers.

The resolution of matters on the British frontier presented Hadrian not only with a problem, but also with a massive opportunity to combine his military and architectural interests. Before considering the extent of his direct involvement in the planning of the Wall, however, we must review our evidence for the chronology of the Wall's origins; can we be certain that it was built under Hadrian's reign?

As we saw in Chapter 1, Hadrian succeeded Trajan in August 117, returning to Rome as emperor in 118. It is assumed that he spent most of the next three years in Rome, consolidating his position. During this time, he must have discussed the situation in Britain with advisers who had first-hand experience of the province, and would surely have begun the development of plans for the British frontier. He set out on his first great imperial inspection of the provinces in 121. This kept him away from Rome for four years, taking him to Gaul, Germany and Britain, then back to Gaul and on to Spain, North Africa, the East, Turkey and Greece. Throughout this tour, he was concerned with the rationalisation of frontiers and the welfare of the army; it is within this context that we must seek the origins of the Wall.

We know that the British Governor, Aulus Platorius Nepos, left Germany to take up his position in Britain in the early summer of 122. It is generally assumed (not unreasonably, but without any clear evidence) that Hadrian travelled with him from Germany to Britain. We don't know how long Hadrian stayed in the province, but (assuming he did arrive with Nepos) it is unlikely to have been more than a dozen or so weeks, as by early 123 he was in North Africa, having travelled via Gaul and Spain. The conventional chronology for the construction of the Wall sees work commencing during Hadrian's visit, to plans developed on site directly by the emperor. Following his departure, work then continued under the direction of Nepos who, as a personal friend of Hadrian, would have liaised closely with him over changes to the initial blueprint. We know from several inscriptions that the Wall was largely completed under Nepos' governorship, which is likely to have ended in 126. For example, two inscriptions from Milecastle 38 (Hotbank), which were presumably set originally over the north and south gates, commemorate the Second Legion Augusta, the governor Aulus Platorius Nepos, and the emperor Caesar Trajan Hadrian Augustus. A fragmentary inscription of similar form from Milecastle 37 (Housesteads) records work by the Second Legion under Nepos, while another from Milecastle 42 (Cawfields) also records Nepos as governor; the full inscription on both of these may have been identical to those from Hotbank milecastle, and it is probable that similar inscriptions were erected over the north and south entrances to every milecastle. From the turf wall, a small fragment of an oak inscription from Milecastle 50 (High House) has been plausibly interpreted as recording the names of Nepos and Hadrian.

In accordance with standard practice, the wording of these inscriptions is abbreviated, and, although the intended original meaning would have been immediately apparent to people in Roman times, interpretation today can sometimes be contentious. A brief lesson in Latin grammar is necessary. The inscriptions from Hotbank milecastle read as follows (letters in brackets are included here though omitted from the actual inscriptions):

IMP(ERATORIS) CAES(ARIS) TRAIAN(I)
HADRIANI AUG(USTI)
LEG(IO) II AUG(USTA)
A(ULO) PLATORIO NEPOTE LEG(ATO) PR(O) PR(AETORE)

The point to stress here is that while most imperial inscriptions were dedicated to or for the emperor, Hadrian's name in this case is given in the genitive, indicating possession, thus suggesting that the Wall should be considered as his own work. Nepos' name is in the ablative, indicating that the work was done under his command. The inscriptions are perhaps best translated as:

> *This, the work of the Emperor Caesar Trajan Hadrian Augustus,*
> *(was built by) the Second Legion Augusta*
> *under Aulus Platorius Nepos, propraetorian legate.*

Thus, these important inscriptions not only confirm the Wall (or at least this part of it) as of Hadrianic date, but also imply the personal involvement of the emperor in the project. Scholars will no doubt continue to debate the exact meaning of the Latin, but for now it seems reasonable to accept this interpretation.

In addition to these inscriptions from milecastles, three inscriptions from forts are fundamental to our dating of the Wall's construction. A dedication slab from a granary at Benwell (*Condercum*) records the construction of the building by *'A vexillation of the British fleet under the governor Aulus Platorius Nepos for the Emperor Caesar Trajan Hadrian Augustus'*. A slab from the west gate of Halton Chesters (*Onnum*) records construction by *'The Sixth Legion Victrix under the governor Aulus Platorius Nepos for the Emperor Caesar Trajan Hadrian Augustus'*. From Great Chesters (*Aesica*) comes an unusual dedication slab, its upper half left blank while the inscription on its lower half can be translated as *'To the Emperor Caesar Trajan Hadrian Augustus, Father of the Country'*. The title *'Pater Patriae'* (usually abbreviated to 'PP', and translated as 'Father of the Country') was officially adopted by Hadrian in 128, so this inscription has been cited as proof that Great Chesters was later in date than most of the Wall forts. Its use has, however, been recorded elsewhere from earlier contexts, prior to Hadrian's official adoption of the title, so it remains possible that the fort predates 128.

When considering these inscriptions it is crucial to bear in mind that they date the completion, and not necessarily the commencement, of construction work at the relevant structures. We still have no clear evidence of the date at which construction work on the Wall began. No Hadrianic inscriptions recording any other governor are known from the Wall, and, while it is not impossible that some may be found in future, the currently available evidence suggests that the Wall complex was largely in place by the end of Nepos' term as governor, that is probably by 126, and certainly by 127.

There must have been many further Hadrianic inscriptions at forts and milecastles along the Wall, and further examples will doubtless be recovered in future. There may also be inscriptions from other monuments awaiting discovery. Two fragments of a particularly fascinating inscription were recovered from the nave of St Paul's Church, Jarrow in 1782. This church, part of the Venerable Bede's monastery, dates originally from the late seventh century, and its builders used much Roman masonry from nearby sites. The fragments recovered in 1782 represent about a quarter of a massive inscription, estimated to have measured 1.8 by 1.5 metres. In the 1940s, the archaeologists Ian Richmond and R P Wright attempted to reconstruct the inscription from the two fragments. Their reconstruction may be translated as:

Son of all the deified emperors, the Emperor Caesar Trajan Hadrian Augustus, after the necessity of keeping the empire within its limits had been laid on him by divine command......once the barbarians had been scattered and the province of Britannia recovered, added a frontier between either shore of the Ocean for 80 miles. The army of the province built the wall under the direction of Aulus Platorius Nepos, Pro-Praetorian Legate of Augustus.

Richmond and Wright believed this inscription to have been set within a huge memorial somewhere near the east end of the Wall. They suggest it may have stood on the north bank of the Tyne estuary, close to where the ruins of Tynemouth Priory stand today, dominating the estuary for anyone sailing up or down the coast, or entering the Tyne. Such a monument would certainly have appealed to Hadrian, whom we may reasonably assume would have designed it himself. Richmond and Wright also suggest that a similar monument would have stood at the west end of the Wall, though no remnant of this has yet been recognised. We do not know what such structures would have looked like, but they would certainly have provided a 'monumental gloss' to the relatively unsophisticated architecture of the Wall, giving the project an altogether more typically Hadrianic character. We may also assume that a monument of some kind, probably a great triumphal gate with appropriate inscription, would have stood at the junction of the Wall and the great north road known to us as Dere Street, and several further commemorative structures probably stood at other strategic locations along the Wall. Perhaps one day we will find inscriptions associated with such monuments, but it is more likely that they have been destroyed; indeed it is miraculous that the two Jarrow fragments survived to provide the only evidence we have for a possible monument at the Wall's east end. This inscription, and the monument of which it formed part, certainly suggest that prestige, rather than simply the construction of a defensive barrier, was a key consideration in the design and construction of the Wall.

Taking all the evidence into account, what can we say about Hadrian's personal involvement in the design of his Wall? As noted earlier, virtually nothing is known for certain, but a reasonable degree of informed speculation is certainly possible. One key question is whether or not Hadrian actually visited the northern frontier. Two altars, dedicated to Neptune and Oceanus, recovered from the Tyne at Newcastle and now on display in the Great North Museum, have been interpreted as personal offerings by Hadrian, perhaps erected on the *Pons Aelius* in imitation of Alexander the Great's sacrifices to the same two gods on the River Hydaspes, at the opposite end of the empire, some four centuries earlier. While undeniably an attractive interpretation of the altars, this is certainly not proven. The very name of the bridge at Newcastle, *Pons Aelius* (the same name as that given to the bridge leading to Hadrian's mausoleum in Rome, discussed in Chapter 1), suggests Hadrian's presence here, as bridges were not normally named in this manner. While neither the bridge nor the altars can be regarded as definite proof that Hadrian was ever personally present at Newcastle, other factors suggest that he must surely have visited the frontier zone during his one and only visit to Britannia in 122.

We know that Hadrian visited the empire's frontiers along the Rhine and the Danube, and in Africa, so it seems reasonable to assume that his visit to Britannia would have included an inspection of the frontier. His interest in military matters would, surely, have led him to spend time mingling with the troops at the northern extremity of the empire, where we may envisage him participating enthusiastically in grand hunting expeditions into the untamed wilderness of the frontier landscape's central sector. There is some intriguing evidence from Vindolanda that suggests Hadrian may have stayed here during his tour of the frontier. Among the many extraordinary writing tablets recovered over recent years by the Vindolanda Trust is one that appears to be a draft of a petition written by a soldier seeking redress for a beating he had suffered at the hands of an officer. Part of this can be translated as:

'I implore your majesty not to allow me, an innocent man, to have been beaten with rods…..as if I had committed some crime'

It is not known to whom this was addressed, but the use of the Latin word *'maiestas'* ('majesty') suggests that it may have been intended for the emperor, and that the man who wrote it had hoped to gain an audience with Hadrian (who, as we have seen, was keen on military discipline but also on fairness). Excavations at Vindolanda in the 1990s uncovered the remains of a large, high-status timber building of some fifty rooms dating from about the time of the imperial visit. This could well have been built specifically for Hadrian and his entourage, as Vindolanda would be the obvious place for him to stay while inspecting the central sector of the frontier. However, whether he actually did stay here, or whether the anonymous petitioner got to speak with him, are likely to remain forever unknown.

While acknowledging that we have no absolute proof of Hadrian's direct involvement in the design of the Wall, it is, I think, highly probable that he did inspect the frontier in person, discuss the situation on the ground with the troops, and play the main role in the conception and design of the Wall. The governor and the army (and especially the legions who undertook most of the construction work) probably welcomed the new project and the opportunity it offered to construct a magnificent new monument to glory of Rome and its leader; glory that would be achieved through architecture rather than warfare. Some decisions would be delegated to the men on the ground, hence the variations in Wall construction, most notably in the form of the milecastles which varied according to which legion they were constructed by, but the direct hand of Hadrian can surely be detected in several unique aspects of the Wall scheme. These unique elements include the overall huge scale of the project and the regularity in its design; the widespread use of stone; the invention of the milecastle; the placing of forts astride the line of the Wall; and the presence of the vallum. These unique elements, none of which is present on other frontiers, surely imply Hadrian's direct involvement in the Wall project, but if the Wall was his idea then was it the original plan or the revised plan (with forts and vallum) for which he was primarily responsible? The answer, I suspect, is both, but how can this be the case if he was only present in the province for two or three months?

A key point to recognise is that Hadrian did not have to be present in the province for work on the Wall to commence, even if the original design was his. His biographer states that Hadrian 'set off for Britain and .... erected a Wall', but this does not preclude a great deal of preparatory work prior to his visit. A recent discovery on the German frontier would certainly seem to suggest that work took place there prior to the imperial visit. As we saw in Chapter 1, Hadrian was on the German frontier in 121/122, prior to his visit to Britain, and it is usually assumed that he initiated the construction of the timber frontier work during this visit. However, recent dendrochronological ('tree-ring') dating demonstrates that timber used in the German frontier palisade came from a tree felled in 119 or 120, clearly suggesting that work was underway here a year or two before Hadrian's visit. If this was the case in Germany, then surely it would also have been the case in Britain.

Prior to his visit, Hadrian must have discussed the British frontier many times with men who had served on it, and would thus have had a good grasp of the frontier landscape. So it is not necessary for him to have visited prior to drawing up the initial plans for the Wall. Indeed, as an architect, he would have relished the potential offered by the wild, northern edge of his empire to attempt something altogether exceptional, and would surely have enjoyed developing some ideas from afar, knowing that he would visit the frontier for himself in due course. We should acknowledge the possibility, however remote, that the original plans for the Wall were the work of the British governor rather than the emperor, and that it was Hadrian who drew up the revised plan. However, it is surely more probable that Hadrian drew up the original blueprint and ordered construction to commence, perhaps as early as 119 or 120, in advance of his visit to the province in 122, subsequently agreeing revisions following consultation with various advisers during his inspection of the frontier. In contrast to the traditional view, that Hadrian's personal inspection of the frontier provided the initial inspiration for the Wall, I think it highly probable that much work on the Wall system had already been completed for him to inspect during his visit. This early work may have included most, if not all, of the turf wall in the west, a substantial length of broad wall in the east, further sections of broad wall including those adjacent to the rivers Irthing and North Tyne, and many milecastles (or at least, their north walls, incorporating observation towers) and turrets. The imperial inspection then resulted in the decision to add the forts and vallum; a decision of such magnitude that it must surely have directly involved the emperor himself. Hadrian was certainly not slow to institute large-scale changes in military logistics when he thought them appropriate. As Cassius Dio observes, possibly with the British frontier in mind:

Hadrian travelled through one province after another, visiting the various regions and cities and inspecting all the garrisons and forts. Some of these he removed to more desirable places, some he abolished, and he also established some new ones.

The decision to reduce the width of the Wall (from broad to narrow) may have come rather later, long after Hadrian's departure from the province (though presumably with his blessing), perhaps as the construction gangs returned to the curtain wall following completion of the forts.

This scenario is, admittedly, based largely on conjecture, but I believe it fits the currently available evidence. Further support for it can be sought in the evidence of so-called 'dislocation', when large-scale changes in the plan can be identified. In his detailed analysis of the Wall, Peter Hill suggests two periods of dislocation. The first, which has long been recognised, occurs at the time when the forts and vallum were added, followed by the reduction in wall-width from broad to narrow gauge. Without entering into the detail of the argument (readers are referred to Hill's book for this), it seems there was something of a relaxation in quality control following this change in plan.

Hill also suggests a second dislocation at some point soon after the forts were begun, where a clear decline in standards can be seen in, for example, the construction of individual gateways at forts and milecastles. The relationship between these two dislocations is not clear and it may be that they are part of a single phenomenon, occurring once Hadrian's visit was over and the 'revised plan' implemented. Hill suggests that the philosophy changed at the dislocations from a desire to produce architecture of good, albeit unsophisticated, quality, to a desire to get the job done as soon as possible. Perhaps Hadrian made this decision himself, though given what we know of his love of architecture this may be considered unlikely. Alternatively, once the emperor's inspection was over, and it became clear that he was most unlikely to return, those on the ground may have decided that speed was of the essence. It is also worth noting that if the Wall was whitewashed (a key aspect of its appearance over which expert opinion remains divided) then variations in construction would be rendered largely invisible.

It has been suggested that the decision to speed up the building process may have been linked to a brief period of warfare, but evidence for this remains ambiguous. Rather, it may have simply been a result of drafting in auxiliary troops to help with the building, all of whom were unskilled in comparison to the legions with their specialist teams of architects and masons. Although the collation of evidence from different sites along the Wall can be frustratingly difficult, it seems reasonable to assume that initial high quality work was begun in several places in preparation for, or during, the imperial inspection of the frontier in the summer of 122, with a decision taken to work faster, but with a loss in quality, following Hadrian's departure.

In Chapter 1, we noted in our discussion of Hadrian's villa at Tivoli that much of the architecture appears experimental, with design changes implemented when construction work was well underway. Clearly, this was also the case with the Wall, a unique and largely experimental project, and perhaps we should see such changes as something of a characteristic of Hadrian's work; plans would be drawn up and construction work implemented, but there was still much scope for change as the emperor observed and contemplated construction in progress.

To summarise, there are a number of reasons for believing that Hadrian was personally responsible for both the initial plan and the revised plan for the Wall. Chief amongst these are:

1. In general terms, the form of the Wall complex is so vast, and so different from anything anywhere else in the empire, that the direct involvement of the emperor in its design seems entirely reasonable,

especially when Hadrian's personal interests in architecture, military matters, and frontier consolidation are taken into account.

2. The original architectural blueprint bears the hallmark of having been designed elsewhere and 'imposed' on the landscape, rather than designed on site by someone personally familiar with the frontier landscape.

3. There was no necessity for Hadrian to be present for work on the Wall to commence, and the available archaeological evidence certainly does not preclude the commencement of construction prior to 122.

4. Hadrian was no fool, and simply would not have made, or authorised, a 'mistake' of the scale implied by the so-called 'fort decision' had he previously inspected the ground for himself. However, had he relied initially from information from advisors, he may have ordered the construction of the Wall, to the original plan, from afar, but always with the intention of visiting and revising the plans as necessary while work was in progress.

5. Much of Hadrian's architectural work may be considered as to an extent experimental; his stunning villa complex at Tivoli being the classic example. He was clearly not afraid to experiment, or to introduce radical changes once projects were underway, as happened during construction of the Wall.

In his comprehensive account of the planning of the Wall, John Poulter considers the evidence for Hadrian's personal involvement in the project, noting that a key weakness in his own speculation is that:

'...all of the ostensibly silly bits are assigned to interference by Hadrian. This is not dissimilar to resorting to the intervention of the Fairy Godmother in a pantomime whenever the going gets tricky.'

This is a fair analogy, but on balance, although we may never know for sure, it seems that Hadrian was, in all likelihood, personally responsible for the Wall's initial blueprint (possibly designed at a desk in Rome), and also (following his personal inspection of the frontier) for the major modification that saw the forts and their garrisons, along with the vallum, added. We will now consider in a little more detail his reasons for building the Wall, including the thinking behind both the initial and revised plans.

2. Why was Hadrian's Wall built?

Having established that Hadrian was, in all probability, personally responsible for the concept of the Wall, we must now ask why he chose to expend such vast resources on its construction, and how it was intended to function. In the 1970s it was estimated that to build the Wall in concrete (the cheapest way) would cost some £80 million, while the costs of building it in stone were simply incalculable; they would have run to many hundreds of millions, regardless of the ditch, vallum, forts and ongoing maintenance costs. From Hadrian's point of view, however, the Wall cost virtually nothing; it was built largely by serving soldiers who had to be paid regardless of whether they were employed on constructing the Wall or some other task, and the raw materials of stone, timber and turf were readily available at no cost to the imperial coffers. That said, the construction was still a huge undertaking, and those involved in the work must have had a clear understanding of what they were doing and why.

It is important to note that Hadrian's Wall did not materialise out of nothing. It was a rationalisation and embellishment of the essentially 'ad hoc' frontier zone that had developed along the Stanegate under Trajan, featuring the forts of Carlisle, Nether Denton, Carvoran, Vindolanda and Corbridge, together with fortlets and forward observation towers. It is generally assumed that Trajan regarded the Stanegate line as a temporary frontier, where his troops would mark time until sufficient resources could be mustered to march north and complete the conquest of the whole island. Clearly, Hadrian thought otherwise, but why the need for such a dramatic alternative when a timber fence was deemed adequate for the German frontier? It is possible that Hadrian was underwhelmed by his experience of the German frontier, and vowed to provide something altogether more appropriate to represent the might of Rome on the northern edge of the empire, representing the northern extremity of the civilised world. Whatever the explanation, we must not lose sight of the fact that the 'Wall' we refer to today was, in its time, much more than just a wall; it was a living frontier system within which thousands of people went about their daily business, the success of which depended on the successful interaction between people and architecture.

When considering the Wall's origin and purpose it is important to observe that its 130km represent in the region of 1% of a frontier system extending more than 10,000km around the entire empire. In the west, the frontier lay along the Atlantic coast, while elsewhere it followed lengths of the North Sea, Black Sea and Red Sea coasts. Given the lack of potential enemies beyond it, the Atlantic coast did not represent much of a threat; indeed it offered much potential for transport and trade, and important settlements grew up at strategic ports in many places.

The North Sea was patrolled by the British fleet, based at Boulogne with further bases at British ports. The north coast of Gaul seems otherwise to have been relatively lightly defended, a situation that was only possible due to Roman occupation of Britannia; had southern Britain not been conquered then the potential threat to the Gaulish coast would have been constant, and this may have been a factor in the decision to occupy the southern half of the island. In short, Roman control of Britannia, and of the Channel, helped to generate and maintain stability in what would otherwise have been a potentially dangerous frontier zone throughout northern Gaul. The province of Britannia was, of course, something of a special case, being surrounded by sea other than to the north, where the Wall that forms the focus of this book provided a barrier linking east and west coasts. In later Roman times the east coast of Britannia was more heavily defended through the addition of what have become known as the 'Saxon Shore forts', and a line of defended towers, presumably for observation, was constructed on the Yorkshire coast. These seem to have been in response to a threat from Saxons and Franks, and they serve to demonstrate the uselessness of the Wall in the face of a threat from a sea-borne enemy.

In the east, the Black Sea, notorious for piracy in Hadrian's time, was patrolled by the Roman Navy which maintained a special Black Sea fleet, and several forts are known around its coasts. These seem to have been linked as much to the management of trade routes as to the defence of the frontier.

Several forts are known along the Egyptian Red Sea coast, all linked by a coastal road known as the *via Hadriana*, for which Hadrian himself may have been responsible. The *via Hadriana* headed inland across the desert to the Nile at Antinoopolis, and could have been designed as parts of Hadrian's plans for this grand new city following the tragic death of Antinous. It provided a link, via the Nile, between the Red Sea coast and the Mediterranean, and may have been intended to help facilitate trade links with the east, as well as improving military communications with troops stationed in the Red Sea frontier forts. Whatever its intended purpose it seems never to have been a busy road, and little is known about it.

North of the Red Sea, the eastern boundaries of the provinces of Arabia and Syria lay along desert frontiers. West of the Red Sea, the African provinces extended southwards to the edge of the Sahara desert. Roman rule in these areas generally only extended over cultivable land, the extent of which was largely dictated by rainfall or, in the case of Egypt, by the Nile. Lines of forts extended along the desert frontiers, with occasional outposts beyond, all located to help manage traditional caravan routes. Roman rule in Africa did not extend everywhere to the fringes of the Sahara, as mountain ranges, most notably the Atlas Mountains, lay north of the desert in some places and these effectively marked the frontier. Mountain ranges also provided the frontier in other places, such as the Pontic Mountains between the Black Sea and the Euphrates, and the Carpathians which defined the province of Dacia. Along all these mountain frontiers, forts were strategically located to control passes and thus to manage the movement of people and goods in and out of the empire.

The empire's north-east frontier, extending from the North Sea to the Black Sea, lay for the most part along the great rivers of the Rhine and the Danube. By Hadrian's time, four legionary bases lay along the Rhine, with nine on the Danube (plus one north of the Danube in the province of Dacia). These bases, at three of which Hadrian had himself served prior to becoming emperor, were carefully located to guard strategic locations. Numerous auxiliary units were also based along this frontier, with some 50% of the empire's entire auxiliary army based on the Danube. In addition, both the Rhine and the Danube were patrolled by dedicated fleets that presumably played a key role in the supply of provisions and equipment to the frontier troops, as well as being constantly 'on call' to deal with any security issues. South of the Black Sea and north of the Syrian desert, the frontier lay for some 250km along a third great river, the Euphrates. Relatively little is known about this stretch of the frontier, but a further four legions were based along it.

In some places, there was no conveniently positioned coast, river, desert or mountain range to act as a frontier. It seems to have been Hadrian who initiated the construction of artificial linear boundaries in these places. The best known example is Hadrian's Wall, linking the east and west coasts of England across the Tyne-Solway isthmus and thus forming the empire's northern frontier. In the gap between the headwaters of the Rhine and the Danube, Hadrian began (but apparently did not complete) a timber palisade known today as the 'Upper German-Raetian *limes*'. It is probably this frontier that the *Historia Augusta* is referring to when noting:

'.....*in many regions where the barbarians are held back not by rivers but by artificial barriers, Hadrian shut them off by means of high stakes planted deep in the ground and fastened together in the manner of a palisade.*'

This was a huge engineering feat, but having been of timber rather than stone it does not capture the public imagination today in the same way as the Wall.

Both Hadrian's Wall and the German limes were constructed through existing frontier zones established by Trajan; the intention in both cases seems to have been to reinforce, and make permanent, the frontier lines. In both cases, however, significant changes were wrought by Hadrian's successor. In Britain, Antoninus built the Antonine Wall from Clyde to Forth, but this was short-lived and Hadrian's Wall became the long-term frontier. In Germany, Antoninus ordered the construction of a new palisade, along with numerous new forts and towers, some 30km east of Hadrian's, and this was duly completed through to the Danube, though apparently not within his lifetime. The relationships between Hadrian's British and German frontier works and those of Antoninus are fascinating, but further discussion lies beyond the remit of this volume.

As we observed in Chapter 1, Hadrian seems also to have been involved in the construction of linear frontier works along parts of the African frontier (known to us as the *Fossatum Africae*), though these remain poorly understood. Even less well understood is the so-called *Limes Transalutanus* which seems to form part of the empire's frontier between the Carpathian mountains and the Danube in the south-east of the province of Dacia. This is also usually ascribed, though on the basis of rather flimsy evidence, to Hadrian.

A fascinating contemporary view of Roman frontier policy is provided by Aelius Aristides, from Mysia on the Aegean coast of Asia Minor, who visited Rome a few years after Hadrian's death and penned his *Roman Oration*, in praise of the city and the empire. In this, he notes that the heart of the empire is effectively demilitarised, with most troops based around the frontiers. Part of his Oration (here translated by J.H. Oliver) reads:

'To place the walls around the city itself as if you were hiding her or fleeing from your subjects you considered ignoble and inconsistent with the rest of your concept, as if a master were to show fear of his own slaves. Nevertheless, you did not forget walls, but these you placed around the empire, not the city. And you erected walls splendid and worthy of you, as far away as possible, visible to those within the circuit, but, for one starting from the city, an outward journey of months and years if he wished to see them.'

Aristides further observes that towns, populated with colonists, were founded along the lines of the frontier, thus extending the 'beautiful order' of Roman civilisation to the furthest reaches of the empire. He continues:

'An encamped army, like a rampart, encloses the civilised world in a ring......from the settled areas of Aethopia to the Phasis, and from the Euphrates in the

interior to the great outermost island towards the west.'

The 'great outermost island' is, of course, Britain. Aristides was not the only author who wrote in praise of the frontier. A contemporary historian named Appian, from Alexandria, notes in his History of Rome that:

'The emperors…..surround the empire with a great circle of camps and guard so great an area of land and sea like an estate'.

Appian provides an interesting explanation as to the location of the static frontier, suggesting the emperors now realised that further expansion would be pointless as all the land worth conquering had now been conquered:

'Possessing the best part of the earth and sea they have, on the whole, aimed to preserve their empire by the exercise of prudence, rather than to extend their sway indefinitely over poverty-stricken and profitless tribes of barbarians.'

Whether Hadrian would have agreed with this must be open to some doubt; his frontier policy seems to have been rooted in common sense, dictated to a large extent by circumstance, and he was well aware that much fertile land, and many wealthy communities that others would consider well worth conquering, existed outside the bounds of the empire. However, whatever the explanation, the frontier was now static, and Hadrian's Wall was part of it. There is much fascinating research to be done on all the frontier zones, before, during, and after Hadrian's reign, and as more work is done it is quite possible that new light will be thrown on the detailed thinking behind Hadrian's Wall. There is no space here, however, for further discussion of frontiers in general; readers wishing to study this subject in more detail should consult David Breeze's excellent *The Frontiers of Imperial Rome*. For now we must refocus our attention on northern England.

Discussions of the intended purposes of the Wall, and the ways in which it was supposed to function, have exercised the minds of many prominent archaeologists over the decades, and will no doubt continue to do so in future. The arguments can be complex, but it seems that Hadrian probably had three separate, but interlinked, reasons for ordering the building of the Wall:

a. The policing of the movement of people through the frontier zone.

b. The provision of a military installation to aid the defence of the province.

c. The construction of a magnificent monument to the glory of Rome on the very edge of the empire.

We will now briefly examine each of these in turn, beginning with the idea of frontier control.

2a. The Wall and frontier control

The Wall was initially planned as a barrier to the movement of people and livestock, but the provision of milecastles at regular intervals demonstrates beyond reasonable doubt that the idea was to control, rather than prevent, such movement. Individuals, groups of men on horseback, farmers with livestock, or indeed large gatherings of warriors, would all be seriously hampered by the Wall, and no doubt any attempt to circumnavigate it by sea to east or west would have to contend with regular patrols by the Roman navy. A concerted assault by a band of warriors at a particular point would, no doubt, result in some of them getting through, or over, the Wall, but to what end? We must assume that the Wall, as originally planned, was to be patrolled in some way, and news of any incursion from the north, however minor, would soon be relayed to troops at the Stanegate forts who would rapidly be on hand to deal with it. The chances of any raiding parties who made it through the Wall escaping back up north, we might note, would also be seriously reduced by the presence of the Wall.

The Wall as originally designed (but, as we have seen, never actually completed), with towers and milecastles, but no forts, was essentially a defensive, or reactive concept. Anyone wishing to pass through it would have to obtain permission from guards at the milecastles, akin to a modern customs post or airport security check, perhaps also paying customs duties or other taxes in order to proceed. We know that frontiers elsewhere in the empire were controlled in this way, with some groups granted unimpeded access while others had to pay duties, for example to pass through a frontier to trade within the empire. The construction of the Wall would certainly have helped to facilitate such frontier management.

In Chapter 2, we noted Erik P. Graafstal's observation that the turf wall in the west, and the broad wall in the east, together with small sections cutting off natural routes through the central sector and, crucially, sections across the main river valleys of the Irthing and the North Tyne, all seem to have been prioritised for early completion in advance of the 'fort decision'. While this might appear a logical approach in the face of hostile groups to the north, it also makes perfect sense in terms of a system to control civilian movement across the frontier, most of which must always have occurred in the lowlands east and west of the wild central sector. This is not to say that a military element was not present within the planning of the earliest phases, it almost certainly was, but the decision to concentrate the earliest phases of construction on natural routes was not necessarily made exclusively on military grounds.

Should any threat be encountered by the Wall guards, they would presumably have been able to call up troops from the forts to the south. Here we must reflect for a moment on the manner in which this new installation was to be garrisoned and patrolled. With no forts along the line, all troops resident on the Wall would have to be stationed in the milecastles and turrets. Although it is possible that a permanent Wall garrison was intended, it is usually assumed that the Wall was to be manned by detachments of troops from the Stanegate forts, perhaps undergoing short tours of duty based in the milecastles and turrets. There would, presumably, also have been regular patrols that left the Stanegate forts to patrol particular lengths of the Wall and areas to the north, before returning to the forts. We may note again here that the width of the broad wall, at ten Roman feet, is only really explicable if a wall-walk was intended, and the presence of regular patrols along the top of the Wall would certainly have added to its effectiveness as a perceived barrier to movement across its line.

The initial blueprint for the Wall called for milecastles at approximately regular intervals, not necessarily at sensible crossing places where existing north-south routes crossed its line. Indeed, some are absurdly positioned if access was the primary consideration; Cawfields is on high ground with a sheer drop to the north, when it could have easily been positioned in an accessible natural gap through the crags just a short distance to the west, and Sewingshields overlooks a sheer drop and may never have had a north gate. Because of this, it is reasonable to assume that the milecastles were designed to play a further role in addition to acting as customs points; this further role was presumably the provision of accommodation for men stationed on the Wall, perhaps in groups of about thirty to each milecastle. The milecastles also seem to have played a key role, along with the turrets, in an intended signalling system linked to the Stanegate forts to the south. Indeed, the relationship between the Stanegate forts and the troops that manned the Wall is crucial to our understanding of the entire complex as originally planned. Recent survey work, discussed in Chapter 2, demonstrates that the alignment of the Wall paid as much if not more attention to views southwards than those to the north (in several places, the line could have been adjusted slightly to provide better views to the north, but this would have precluded a clear view back to the Stanegate). Detailed analysis of the location of the milecastles and turrets suggests that, while the basic blueprint called for a structure every third of a Roman mile, there was an acceptable degree of variation in this layout to enable structures to have views back to the Stanegate (in some cases by way of intermediate signal towers) and thus for some kind of signalling system to have been in operation.

This view gains further support from the fact that the Wall incorporates at least two earlier towers, at Walltown Crags and Pike Hill, that must originally have been observation towers linked to Stanegate forts (Walltown to Carvoran fort, and Pike Hill to Nether Denton fort). However, there is something of a problem here in that the Stanegate has not been traced east of Corbridge or west of Carlisle, so how these lengths of Wall were intended to relate to troops garrisoned to the south remains a mystery. It is possible that further sites remain to be discovered, or that a different system was planned to operate either side of the central sector. Alternatively, if the original plan was primarily about frontier control, then a need to get substantial numbers of troops to any point on the Wall at very short notice may not have been a primary concern; an efficient signalling system along the Wall that also linked with the Stanegate forts to the south may have been deemed quite adequate.

The native people in the Wall corridor, at least towards its east end, are referred to by the Romans as the Brigantes. The Brigantes, probably a loose affiliation of independent chiefdoms, seem to have preferred a traditionally 'barbarian' way of life, shunning the processes of Romanisation adopted by tribes further south. The Roman administrative capital for the Brigantian territory, *Isurium Brigantium*, at Aldborough in Yorkshire, was apparently founded during Hadrian's reign but never grew into a large or prosperous town like other Roman capitals. Traditional Brigantian territory probably extended a long way north of the Wall, and close links may have existed with tribes even further north; it is likely that the Brigantes were linked in some way to the conflict recorded at the time of Hadrian's accession. It may well be, therefore, that part of Hadrian's thinking in building the Wall was to regulate movement within Brigantian territory. Perhaps Hadrian founded Aldborough as a positive new focus to encourage Romanisation in this potentially troublesome region, at the same time as building the Wall to discourage relations with hostile neighbours to the north. The admittedly limited evidence currently available does suggest that many native settlements north of the Wall were abandoned during the second century, while a number of villas are known from as far north as County Durham. Taken together this evidence might suggest that a large-scale reorganisation of settlement throughout the entire frontier zone occurred soon after the construction of the Wall; this suggestion is further considered later in this chapter.

In the west, the outpost forts suggest that substantial areas north of the Wall may have been effectively under Roman control, though it was not practical to extend the Wall around them. The same was probably true in the east, though the outpost forts here seem, on present evidence, to have post-Hadrianic origins. Although tribal boundaries are not known for certain, we know that the land north of the Wall in the east was occupied by the generally pro-Roman Votadini, but in the west the Novantae and Selgovae are thought to have posed serious problems for the Romans, potentially playing a role in the frontier conflict recorded early in Hadrian's reign. This may have been a factor in the decision to complete the turf wall as a priority in the west, linked to the outpost forts. Normal Roman procedure in such frontier regions was to manage the local population through a combination of carrot and stick; treaties, sometimes linked to payments, were preferential to war, but any 'disagreement' could soon be settled through swift and decisive military action. In some cases lands beyond the frontiers became 'buffer states' – nominally independent but with leaders closely allied to (and in some cases dependent upon) Rome. Direct Roman administration thus extended only as far as the frontier, but Roman influence extended far beyond. This may well have been the case with the Votadini during Hadrian's reign, but a similar arrangement in the west may not have been possible.

The Wall in the west extended to the lowest fording point across the Solway, at Bowness. Clearly the intention here was also to control movement across the line. South-west of Bowness, the line of milefortlets and turrets, perhaps linked by a palisade, extending down the coast was similarly intended to enable observation and control of movement. The chronology of this coastal system is not fully understood, but it is thought to have formed part of the original 'grand design'.

What is clear is that along the entire length of the Wall, as originally planned, there was not a garrison of a size capable of repelling any concerted attempt to cross it. It was not intended as a military barrier to repel an invading army, but as an aid to the control of movement in both directions through the frontier zone. Following the 'fort decision', troops garrisoned along the line of the Wall presumably undertook regular patrols along it, and the link to the Stanegate became less significant. The implications of this change are considered further in the next section, but we should note here that the milecastles remained in service, so the Wall continued to function as originally intended even though the vallum, to the south, now restricted access through the Wall complex to a greater extent that the original plan.

Its sheer size demonstrates that the Wall was intended as a long-term installation; Hadrian had deemed that the frontier would remain here for a long time, if not forever. The Wall was probably never intended as a line to demarcate the exact 'edge of empire', but was planned to run through the heavily militarised frontier zone. Its primary practical function would seem to have been to help control movement through this zone. Rather than a direct response to a perceived military threat, it was probably built as an aid to security and control across what was, already, conquered and largely pacified territory. In other words, it was intended as an aid to the security of the frontier, and an enticement for Roman civilisation to expand into the lands to its south, not primarily as a military barrier to be defended against hordes of warriors from 'up north'. In this respect, the *Historia Augusta* is correct in noting that Hadrian had conceived it 'to force apart the Romans and barbarians'.

2b. The Wall as a military installation

The original plan for the Wall, discussed above, may have been primarily about controlling the movement of civilians across its line, rather than repelling attacks by hostile armies, but the Wall is nevertheless a military monument. It was built by the military, and in the absence of a specialist police or customs force, was manned by soldiers. Following the decision to place the forts along its line, it became a more overtly aggressive military installation, no longer dependent on troops stationed to the south along the Stanegate. It is not possible to overstress the change that overcame the Wall through the decision to build the Wall forts; it completely changed in character and evolved into a thoroughly different beast from that described above. While the everyday life of the Wall garrison must have been based largely around training and routine patrolling, probably both along the Wall and throughout the lands to the north, the ability to deal with any potential threat approaching from the north was now clear for all to see.

We noted, above, that the Wall was not built in an orderly fashion from one end to the other, but that some sectors seem to have been prioritised from the start. These include the turf wall in the west, the long stretch of broad wall between Dere Street and Newcastle in the east, and stretches of broad wall across the rivers Irthing and North Tyne. While acknowledging that these would have helped to control civilian movement across the frontier, they could also have played a role in intercepting any bands of warriors, or even large armies, who would naturally have chosen one of these routes into the province from the north. It is therefore not unreasonable to assume that the military defence of the province was a key factor in the design of the Wall from the outset, despite the fact that no forts were initially located along its line. We know from the *Historia Augusta* that there was conflict in Britain at the start of Hadrian's reign, in 117, and assume that this was primarily the result of incursions from the north. Hadrian responded by sending his friend, the celebrated general Quintus Pompeius Falco, to sort out the British frontier, a task promptly accomplished, probably in 118. It is interesting to note that if this conflict involved fighting in what is now Scotland, which it probably did, then it was the only military campaign of any great consequence that Hadrian fought *outside* the bounds of the empire throughout his entire reign. This conflict may well have contributed to the idea of the Wall, but the Wall would take several years to construct, and it seems that unrest continued to simmer in the north, breaking out into further warfare in 123 or 124, while construction of the Wall was underway. Our evidence for these 'British wars' is sketchy, consisting essentially of a couple of inscriptions from Italy recording the careers of senior officers who served in an *'expeditio Britannica'* ('British expedition'), probably in 123 or 124, the tombstone of a centurion from Vindolanda who was 'killed in the war', and coins that seem to commemorate military victories in 118 and 124. Two coin hoards from Birdoswald, apparently deposited in about 123, while the fort was under construction, along with another of similar date from near Vindolanda, have been interpreted as evidence of conflict at this time; they were presumably concealed in a hurry and, for whatever reason, their owners never returned to recover them. This evidence alone may not suggest large-scale conflict, but four decades later Marcus Cornelius Fronto (writing in the reign of Marcus Aurelius) refers back to substantial losses suffered under Hadrian at the hands of the Britons. So, while our evidence remains sketchy, it is reasonable to assume that military defence against a substantial northern foe was a key factor underlying the planning of the Wall.

We don't know much about the organisation of the Wall garrison, either as proposed for the initial plan or once the forts were added. One thing we can be absolutely certain of, however, given his well-documented concerns with military discipline, is that Hadrian would have given as much thought to the arrangement of the garrison as to the architecture of the Wall. It was the effective combination of people and architecture that made the system work; the Wall would have been useless without an effective garrison. As discussed in Chapter 2, it appears that the original plan was for a small garrison of some thirty or forty men in each milecastle with perhaps half-a-dozen in each turret (assuming these were continuously manned), linked by some sort of signalling system to the fort garrisons along the Stanegate. The decision to add the forts changed this arrangement profoundly. Earlier in this chapter, it was suggested that Hadrian realised, on visiting the frontier, that his original plans, drawn up from afar, were impractical, and that forts on the line of the Wall were far preferable from a military viewpoint, even if they did mess up his immaculate architectural plans somewhat. Ever the pragmatist, he would have ordered the amendment of his plans if he could see the benefits to his loyal troops on the ground. The alternative suggestion, that he ordered the original plan *after* seeing the frontier for himself, seems inconceivable; he would surely not have made such a poor decision after inspecting the frontier at first hand in the company of his generals. Alternatively, he may always have intended for the forts to be added at some point. The apparent absence of forts north of the Tyne between Corbridge and Newcastle, and our lack of evidence for the Stanegate west of Carlisle, mean we have no idea how the eastern and western sectors of the frontier were meant to be garrisoned in the 'initial plan', within which the central sector was apparently linked with the Stanegate forts. Perhaps the best explanation is that the intent to add the forts was there from the start, though their exact locations were not determined until construction of the Wall was well underway.

We noted earlier that while the Wall was built by the legions, it was garrisoned by auxiliary units. Once the Wall was built, the legions retired to their bases in York, Chester and Caerleon, reflecting the provisional position of the frontier during an earlier stage of the conquest. The legions were always there in reserve, and could be called upon if the Wall was threatened, as indeed were numerous other auxiliary units stationed at forts throughout the frontier zone. Auxiliary units were founded in numerous places throughout the provinces, and retained names reflecting their places of origin even though they could be stationed anywhere within the empire. As time went by these units recruited locally so that ties with their original homelands became gradually less significant. Thus, for example, the Second Cohort of Nervians (originally from Belgium), known to have been present at Wallsend, Vindolanda and Whitley Castle at various times, probably included many native Brigantes after it had been here for two or three generations. In addition to the auxiliary units there were, from the mid-second century and possibly earlier, irregular units of non-citizen troops known as *numeri* that helped to man the Wall. The origin of the *numeri* is not known for sure, but they may have been set up by Hadrian specifically to provide cheap but reliable forces to help man the frontiers. They were drawn from numerous different places within the provinces and beyond the frontiers. From the later second century we have records of units known as *explorates*, specialist scouts, some of whom were based at outpost forts and whose role must have included patrolling the land north of the Wall. Some such units may have been based at wall forts, possibly also occupying the milecastles. Later still, in the fourth century, we have records of *areani*, who seem to have been secret agents or spies that travelled long distances to the north in search of intelligence; they were disbanded in the later fourth century after some of them had apparently become double agents, betraying the Romans. Whatever the detailed arrangements, regular patrols, and more subversive intelligence gathering, must surely have been prime functions of the Wall garrison as information about what was going on 'up north' would have been crucial to the management of the frontier. To quote J.C. Mann:

'No army can operate effectively without intelligence. But the garrison could not obtain useful information by standing on Hadrian's Wall, peering through the Scotch mist'.

As we saw in Chapter 2, the disposition of auxiliary troops along the Wall was far from random, with cavalry units positioned alongside the main roads and an emphasis on infantry in the more wild landscapes of the central sector. The most senior officer on the Wall was the commander of the *Ala Petriana*, the cavalry unit at Stanwix, the largest of the wall forts, but whether or not this officer, or anyone else, assumed overall command of the entire Wall complex and its garrison of perhaps 10,000 men is not known. Questions as to how the different fort garrisons interacted with each other, and with men stationed in milecastles or turrets, seem unlikely ever to be answered for certain, but we can be certain that Hadrian would have considered such matters carefully and instituted what he considered to be the most appropriate system. Although the military way (the road sandwiched between the Wall and the vallum, linking the various installations along the line) is usually regarded as post-Hadrianic, there must surely have been some lateral transport link along the line of the Wall from the start, perhaps originally a system of tracks rather than a well-engineered road. This would enable the rapid deployment of troops to any point along the frontier complex if required, effectively transforming a potentially weak frontier into a dynamic feature of considerable value to the management of the entire frontier zone. The Roman army would not be caught out through an inability to pass laterally along the frontier, as the English army would be in the eighteenth century.

While we may reasonable question the extent to which northern tribes could ever have genuinely threatened the properly garrisoned province, there can be no doubt that they were considered a threat potentially capable of causing a great deal of damage, if only on a temporary basis. It is interesting to speculate as to whether this threat may have been exaggerated in order to justify the Wall, but this is another question to which we will never have a firm answer.

We will never know exactly why the decision was taken to locate more troops on the line of the Wall, but it may have been the desire to transform an essentially reactive, defensive installation into something altogether more proactive and aggressive, with the potential to deploy thousands of men and cavalry to the north at a moment's notice. Whatever the explanation, the decision necessitated much further construction work, including, in some places, the demolition of partly built stretches of Wall and the infilling of already dug stretches of the ditch. The Roman army prided itself on its mobility, and the restriction of access through the Wall to the milecastles may have created more problems than it solved for the men charged with safeguarding the frontier. Several of the forts added to the line had three massive double gates opening to the north, enabling the rapid deployment of forces here should they be required. While most men leaving these gates would have been on routine patrols, the opportunity was there for them to pass rapidly *en masse* to the north if required, rather than forming an orderly queue to pass through a milecastle. No doubt the Wall still functioned as a 'customs barrier', but the aggressive statement of intent was now clear for all (whether north or south of it) to see.

It seems that some forts elsewhere in northern England were abandoned at the time the wall forts were commissioned; presumably their garrisons were relocated to the Wall. We should also note that the regiments garrisoned at forts in the Wall's central sector were infantry, suitable for patrolling the Wall and the rugged land to its north on foot. To east and west of the central sector, garrisons included cavalry, implying (unless we allow for horses galloping along the wall-top) that their mission was not simply to safeguard the Wall itself but to patrol the wide expanses of land beyond. Clearly, this relationship of cavalry to infantry was part of the grand master plan for the frontier as a whole. Perhaps the main perceived threat was deemed to be across the relatively unpopulated wastes of the central sector, rather than the agricultural, settled lands to east and west; this would explain why infantry regiments were concentrated in the central sector where the landscape was unsuitable for cavalry.

Unsurprisingly, the links back to the Stanegate forts, such a key feature of the original plan, seem unimportant once the troops are moved up onto the Wall. Perhaps the clearest example of this is at Birdoswald, where the original turf wall was carefully aligned with views back to the south, but when this was rebuilt in stone, with the great wall fort of Birdoswald now in place (or at least under construction), it took a new line to the north, giving better views northwards but losing the southerly views that the turf wall had enjoyed. Clearly, these old views southwards were now irrelevant; the original scheme that demanded them was now redundant.

The conventional, popular view of the Wall sees it as a defensible structure, with Roman soldiers fighting from on top of it to repel hoards of invading northern savages. As we have seen, there is no clear proof that the Wall had a walkway, though it seems very likely that it did. Assuming that it did, it is most unlikely that it was ever intended to function primarily as a fighting platform as this is simply not the way the Roman army fought its battles. Furthermore, the limited access to the wall top would have hindered any defending force that had to mount it in a hurry to fight an approaching enemy. It is estimated that about a third of the province's entire auxiliary forces were based along the Wall, but the aim was not for these men to fight from atop the Wall or (as has been seriously suggested) to rush out of two adjacent milecastles and destroy an enemy in a 'pincer movement' against the Wall's north face. Rather the troops were based here to undertake regular patrols of the region to the north, as well as presumably along the Wall. If a threat was perceived then it would be dealt with out in the open field, well north of the Wall. The effectiveness of the Wall thus relied more upon an effective garrison than on the actual structure itself, and, in return, the Wall may well have played a useful psychological role as a 'safe' structure for men to retire back to it after a mission to the north, helping to generate a sense of security and well-being for those stationed upon and behind it.

The Wall was a military monument, built and manned by the army, but it was never intended to play any kind of front-line role on the battlefield, a fact reinforced by its location in relation to the rivers Tyne, Irthing and Eden. In several places the line runs to the north of these rivers, whereas, if its primary purpose was the provision of a defensive barrier, it would surely have run along the south bank, thus utilising the rivers as natural 'moats'. If the Wall was ever approached by an enemy of any size then the system had already failed, though it is undeniably true that the Wall might help to provide a 'last ditch' obstacle to enable such a situation to be rectified. Indeed, the recent recognition of 'cippi' on the berm cold be used to argue that the Wall was intended to function as a fighting platform, though perhaps only as a last resort, if an enemy did manage to approach it.

The most puzzling element of the Wall complex, the vallum, was apparently created as part of the scheme to add the forts to the Wall. The fact that the vallum strides across the landscape in long straight sections, apparently laid out from the forts and paying little attention to views in any direction, suggests that its primary function was the demarcation of a 'military zone' along the south side of the Wall, inaccessible to anyone without the relevant permission. Other than the Portgate on Dere Street, and one or two other possible exceptions, access to this military zone from the south was now restricted to gateways adjacent to the Wall forts. Many of the milecastles seem to have remained in commission, but anyone passing through them could only now pass south out of this military zone via one of the vallum gates. The vallum may have incorporated a track on its north berm linking the milecastles to the gates south of the forts, but this remains unproven. As explained in Chapter 2, the investment in the creation of the vallum was huge, a fact which appears strange to us given our inability to fully understand its purpose. Much of the reasoning behind it may have been to do with the psychology of the troops on the ground, now able to function within a defended corridor within which, in the normal course of events, they would not be distracted by either friendly civilians or those with more sinister intent. (Note that recent events in Afghanistan, and elsewhere, demonstrate that telling the two apart is not always easy, or indeed possible, until serious and often tragic damage has been done).

It has been suggested that the vallum may always have been intended as a temporary structure, created while work on the Wall itself was temporarily halted for some reason. This seems unlikely, as it would have taken arguably less effort to have simply completed the Wall in the first place. Despite the vast resources, in terms of manpower, allocated to its construction, however, the vallum does seem to have had only a brief effective life. The fort at Carrawbrough, probably built in about 130, overlies a flattened sector of the vallum which was not re-built to the south of the fort; the perceived function of the vallum here must, therefore, have already been redundant by this time. The vallum was clearly an experimental aspect of the Wall project, and one that seems to have been shortlived; much of it seems not to have been maintained after the return from the Antonine Wall in the 160s. Although it may appear to us to have been an expensive waste of effort, we should recall that the labour allocated to its construction was effectively free; if not involved in fighting, patrolling or training, the troops could be allocated to construction projects at effectively no cost. (That said, there seems never to have been a decision to flatten the vallum, which could potentially have rendered the land it crosses more useful, if only for agriculture, so perhaps parts of it did retain a practical function for longer than the currently available field evidence might suggest).

In short, the revised plan, while retaining a role in passport and customs control, was for an aggressively orientated and heavily garrisoned military installation, facing north towards any potential enemies while also being delimited, and to an extent protected, by the vallum in the south. Whatever Hadrian's reasoning, we may assume that the troops were happier with this arrangement than with the original, altogether more defensive, proposal. Finally, we should never lose sight of the fact that the military defence of the province certainly did not depend upon the Wall, which never existed in isolation; it was a part, albeit a rather big part, of a military frontier zone extending over much of what is now northern England and southern Scotland which must have been regularly and effectively patrolled using the network of roads, forts and other installations. The way in which the Wall functioned must have been closely integrated with other activity, both military and civilian, throughout this zone.

2c. The Wall as symbolic architecture

Attempts to account for the form of Hadrian's Wall by reference to practical military tactics and/or everyday techniques of frontier management (as discussed above) are fundamentally flawed as they fail to grasp the essential nature of the project. This is not say that such matters were not critical aspects of the project – they were. But the single most important factor in the planning of the Wall was surely Hadrian's obsession with architecture. We saw many examples of this in Chapter 1. In Rome, Athens and elsewhere, Hadrian never missed an opportunity to make a statement through architecture, and the wild, windswept hills on the northern fringe of his great empire provided just such an opportunity. Therefore, leaving aside the practical considerations of how the Wall 'worked', we must also consider its symbolic role as an extraordinary architectural project.

J.C. Mann, in a brief but influential paper published in 1990, describes the Wall as '...a magnificent piece of rhetoric, a rather grandiose statement designed to impress rather than to convey the truth'. He further notes:

'The fact is, of course, that Hadrian wished to make a statement to the people of northern Britain. He wished to state that Rome is invincible: there is no point in your making pin-prick attacks on its invulnerability. Look at this magnificent structure – defended gateways every mile, and turrets with equally imposing regularity. This is pure rhetoric. This is a simple statement of the might of Rome. What hope have you of challenging it?'

It was suggested above that the original blueprint for the Wall, with its regular arrangement of milecastles and turrets, was imposed on the landscape from afar, and that the revised plan, with forts and vallum, followed the detailed inspection of the line, and consideration of various practical matters, when construction work was underway. For various reasons, it is reasonable to believe that both the original decision and the revised plan owed much to the personal involvement of Hadrian himself. Why should he have paid so much attention to what was going on here, so far away from the glories of Rome and Athens?

For those who have read Chapters 1 and 2 of this book the answer should be relatively straightforward. Hadrian saw, in the British frontier, a unique opportunity to build what was effectively the largest artificial structure in the world. He understood as well as anyone the power of architecture, and sought to use this in numerous different theatres throughout the empire. He would also have been well aware of the potential ridicule, both in his own time and subsequently, if he was to get such a huge project horribly wrong. This is why so much effort was put into the original design, and also into the redesign following the decision to add the forts. As we saw in Chapter 1, Hadrian sought the consolidation of frontiers rather than further expansion of the empire's borders. The Wall was designed as a huge statement of this new attitude, not as a defensive apology for the lack of military aggression, but as a triumphant, forward-looking monument that dominated the landscape and left no-one in any doubt that northern Britannia was now permanently part of the mighty Roman Empire. We can argue about the quality of the Wall's architecture; as we have seen, much of it was of no great quality, and an adequate explanation for the original construction of the western sector in turf remains elusive, but much of the grandeur of the Wall lies in its sheer scale. Nothing remotely like it had ever been seen before anywhere in the Roman world, never mind on the wild northern frontier. From our twenty-first century standpoint, attempts to try and imagine the power and symbolism enshrined in the structure of the Wall, and recreate the ways in which this was experienced by local people, is difficult if not impossible. However, there can be no doubt that people, whatever their political views, must have been hugely impressed as they watched the Wall rise before their eyes.

Although rarely commented upon, the form of the Wall may owe something to Hadrian's love of all things Greek. He would have been familiar with Greek walls, such as the 5km long double barrier, with internal towers and fortified gateways, that joined Athens with its harbour, Piraeus. He would also have been aware of the ancient Greek tradition of building defensive works 'to wall out barbarians'. Could it be that his desire was to place a magnificent monument to the glory of ancient Greece at the northern edge of his empire? Regardless of this, the Wall stood as a reminder to everyone that Hadrian himself had shown interest in this land, visiting it and lavishing resources upon it to prove, forever, that it was an important part of his empire. As we have seen above, the Wall played an important practical role in the management of the frontier, but we should never forget that its symbolic role, as a statement of Hadrian's frontier policy, was also a key factor underlying its initial construction and subsequent development.

In assessing Hadrian's reasons for building the Wall, we should always bear in mind that he was, himself, an experienced military man and always enjoyed a positive relationship with the army. In ordering the troops to construct the Wall, he would have been aware that he was giving them a chance to build a great monument that would be regarded with awe by current and future generations. The construction work was hard, but the men pulled together in what must have been generally regarded as a communal project to the glory of the emperor and the empire, as well as a practical structure to aid the management of the frontier. Most probably preferred this to the alternative of putting their lives on the line fighting battles in and around the Scottish highlands, and in the longer term a stable frontier was clearly of value to everyone living south of it.

Once the Wall was built, it was only of value as long as it was efficiently manned. Today we see the ruins of a stone wall, but that wall was no more than a skeleton providing part of the framework for the frontier; the real strength of the frontier was the men who manned it. To these men, the Wall was a positive symbol of Roman strength, a reminder that this wild frontier was part of the great empire centred on the eternal city of Rome. The psychology of the Wall was thus aimed not just at civilians living north and south of it, but also at the men who built and served on it. The psychological impact of patrolling along, and surveying from, an elevated walkway, high above the lands to the north, must have been profound, to both the surveyors and the surveyed. A regularly patrolled road, along with observation towers, would perhaps have done the job adequately, but how much more inspirational to provide a road up in the air, from which the land, and the people on it, could be looked down upon from on high.

The vallum must also be understood in terms of its psychological value rather than simply in practical terms. Its practical purpose, though not fully understood, must have been primarily to demarcate the southern edge of a 'military zone' between it and the Wall. Something more mundane would have done the job quite adequately (the same applies to an extent to the Wall itself), but instead an outrageously massive architectural project was demanded. As with the Wall, this gave the troops a project on which to focus their energies for the glory of the empire, but when in operation, as suggested in the previous section, it must have been of considerable psychological benefit to those garrisoned on the Wall. More fieldwork is needed to enable us to understand the chronology and purpose of the vallum, but, whatever the results of such work, it is hard to see how the its practical value can have been in any way commensurate with the vast resources allocated to its construction and maintenance. As with the Wall, the explanation surely has as much to do with psychology as to practical frontier operations.

When seeking to interpret the Wall we must always bear in mind that only a fraction of the original Hadrianic structure survives today. It is perhaps not unreasonable, on the basis of the surviving remains, to suggest that the Wall may have been a purely practical construction, built out of necessity to help provide a degree of control at the empire's northern extremity. The military architecture of the forts, milecastles and turrets is nothing particularly special, and the Wall itself (whether or not it was originally whitewashed, and regardless of whether it incorporated a walkway) is itself of no great architectural merit. The facts that Hadrian never returned to inspect it, that there are no known contemporary references to it, no coins struck to commemorate it, and (as far as we know) no architectural reference to it in the grounds of the great villa at Tivoli, might be taken to suggest that it was not of as much concern to Rome as we like to think. I suspect, however, that it was always regarded by those who served on it as something special.

This suggestion that the Wall was regarded as special in Roman times receives support from three small bronze 'pans', thought to be second-century souvenirs of the Wall, either purchased by visitors or presented to soldiers who had served on it. The first of these to be discovered is the Rudge Cup, found in 1725 in a well on the site of a Roman villa in Wiltshire; it is now on display in the Duke of Northumberland's museum at Alnwick Castle. The Rudge Cup is decorated with a schematic representation of the Wall, and inscribed with the names of five Wall forts: from the west, MAIS (Bowness), ABALLAVA (Burgh-by-Sands), UXELODUNUM (Stanwix), CAMBOGLANNA (Castlesteads) and BANNA (Birdoswald). A similar object, known as the Amiens Skillet (or Amiens Patera) was found at Amiens in France in 1949. This also adds a sixth fort, ESICA (otherwise known as '*Aesica*'), known to be Great Chesters, east of Birdoswald. The third such object, found as recently as 2003, in Staffordshire, is in many ways the most interesting. Known as the 'Staffordshire Moorlands Patera' (or 'Staffordshire Pan'), it is beautifully decorated in an abstract curvilinear style, based on native Celtic art, and lists four forts; from the west, MAIS (Bowness), COGGABATA (Drumburgh), VXELODVNVM (Stanwix), and CAMMOGLANNA (Castlesteads). The reasons for the different fort names on the three pans need not concern us here, but what is of very great relevance to our discussion is the rest of the inscription on the Staffordshire Pan. The full inscription (which can be read as commencing either with 'MAIS' or 'RIGORE' – the resulting translations being of no significant difference) reads:

MAIS COGGABATA VXELODVNVM CAMBOGLANNA RIGORE VALI AELI DRACONIS

The latter part of this inscription is open to alternative interpretations, but the most likely original meaning is thought to be '*According to the line of the Aelian frontier. By the hand (or the property) of Draco*'. We don't know who 'Draco' was – he may have been the person who made the pan, or the person for whom it was made, but this is of little consequence. The key words to the present discussion are '*VALI AELI*', which imply that the Wall system was known during the second century as '*Vallum Aeli*' - the Aelian frontier. Aelius is of course Hadrian's family name – so the frontier was effectively 'Hadrian's frontier'. We will never know for sure how this name came into being, but few things were named after serving emperors in this way (*Pons Aelius* – Hadrian's bridge at Newcastle - is the only other known local example), so we may reasonably assume that this official title had the blessing of the man himself. The three pans (of which many more examples presumably once existed, some of which may well still await rediscovery) demonstrate that the British frontier was regarded as something very special, and the Staffordshire Pan certainly suggests that it was generally regarded as Hadrian's handiwork.

While the Wall undeniably had practical value in frontier management, Hadrian surely intended it to function, above all, as a magnificent piece of Roman rhetoric. He may also have hoped that it would stand in perpetuity as a reminder of his architectural prowess. The Staffordshire Pan suggests that it achieved this during his lifetime and beyond; indeed, it could be argued that its ruins continue to function in this way today.

Section 3
Architectural Masterpiece or Monument to Failure?
Assessing the long-term effectiveness of Hadrian's Wall.

In the previous section, we attempted to reconstruct Hadrian's thinking in building the Wall, suggesting that he had three interlinked objectives in ordering its construction: frontier control, military defence of the province, and the construction of a great monument to the glory of Rome (and arguably also of himself). Here, we will attempt to analyse the extent to which the Wall met these objectives, both during Hadrian's lifetime and subsequently.

Today, few would dispute the fact that Hadrian's Wall justifies its World Heritage Site status, and most tourists who visit the area are suitably impressed by the quantity and scale of ruins set out for their perusal. Available interpretation stresses the efficiency and the power of the Roman army, power that we can still feel today embedded in the very fabric of the Wall. But despite what all the Romanists tell us about the might of the empire and the wonders of Rome, what was the ultimate factor behind the building of the Wall? Quite simply it was the failure of Rome and her mighty army, for whatever reason, to conquer Scotland. Had Scotland fallen to the legions (which it very nearly did, and surely would have done had successive emperors not been engaged in other priorities) then nobody would ever have contemplated the bizarre notion of building a massive wall for 80 miles from coast to coast across the centre of Britain. It could, therefore, be argued that the Wall, from its very inception, was something of a 'monument to failure' on the part of the Roman authorities. This, however, is not something for which Hadrian can be held responsible.

Hadrian's Wall was built as a response to a number of factors, some empire-wide and some peculiar to Britain. It was one part of a grand scheme which sought to locate the bulk of the army around the fringes of the empire. The fact that the Wall was never entirely abandoned by Rome for as long as the province of Britannia was retained suggests that it must have had a perceived usefulness in the eyes of succeeding emperors. Indeed, the Wall could be regarded as representative of an extremely radical and praiseworthy attempt by Hadrian to consolidate the edges of his empire along sensible and sustainable boundaries. Some authorities (following Appian, quoted earlier) explain this about-turn in Roman frontier policy by suggesting that all the land that was worth conquering had been conquered by Hadrian's time, but this argument is not really valid. It is probably fair to credit Hadrian with the move from an aggressive 'foreign policy' to one of consolidation, and he may well have done this for what we would regard as highly commendable reasons. Having deprived himself of the chance to seek glory through the traditional route of military conquest, he felt driven to seek personal glory elsewhere, and his impressive architectural achievements surely represent part of this quest.

As part of his plans to consolidate the empire, Hadrian gave up some of Trajan's recently conquered territories in the east, and he may have considered giving up Britain and formalising the boundary of the empire along the Channel coast. However, most of England had effectively been 'Roman' for the best part of a century by this time, so to simply 'hand it back to the natives' was not a realistic option, and given his non-expansionist frontier policy, any new attempt to conquer Scotland was firmly off the agenda. On balance he must have decided that the permanent division of the island into a Roman south and a barbarian north was the optimum solution. The Wall was a neat element of this solution, especially as it provided a unique opportunity for some radical architecture. In this context we might recall from Chapter 1 that Hadrian had something of a habit of generating architectural responses to problematic situations. When Antinous died in Egypt, part of Hadrian's response was to build a fantastic new city – Aninoopolis. In Judaea, he sought to demonstrate Roman power over the Jews by rebuilding Jerusalem as a Roman colony and replacing the ancient Jewish temple with a fabulous new temple to Jupiter Capitolinus. Seen in this context, the Wall could be interpreted as a typically Hadrianic 'architectural solution' to a problem.

When considering the 'specialness' of the Wall, however, we should be careful; it may not necessarily have appeared quite as special to those who built and manned it as it does to us today. It may come as a surprise to many tourists visiting Hadrian's Wall to learn that there are no contemporary sources relating to its original construction. And, of course, Hadrian, despite his love of travel, never returned to view the finished product, which we might reasonably have expected him to do if it really meant a great deal to him. Could it be that the Wall was never actually as critical to the defence of the empire as most people today assume it to have been?

3a. The Wall and the military

Hadrian's Wall was a key element within the extensive military zone considered necessary to defend the province of Britannia. Economically, the expense involved in the maintenance of this military zone, coupled with the need to keep the northern tribes quiet through a combination of threat and bribery, was immense. This expense could have been avoided through either a concerted effort to conquer the whole island, or the abandonment of Britannia which, despite its great mineral wealth and agricultural potential, was arguably never an essential element of the empire. Roman frontier policy in Britain could be deemed successful in that it enabled southern England to become 'Romanised', but the need to constantly maintain a substantial military presence in northern England and southern Scotland meant that the conventional public view of a civilised and peaceful Roman society extending up to the Wall, with the 'barbarians' held at bay to the north, was never the case. Instead there was always a substantial military zone between the 'civilised south' and the 'native north'.

It could legitimately be questioned whether the Wall was ever intended to demarcate the actual edge of the empire. Clearly, Roman influence extended to the north, where some areas may have been nominally independent client kingdoms with their own leaders, albeit ultimately subservient to Rome. It may be that the generally pro-Roman tribal kingdoms to the immediate north of the Wall were considered as some kind of 'buffer zone' between the province and the anti-Roman northern tribes. Perhaps the people of southern Scotland actually welcomed the building of the Wall, seeing it as ensuring their (perceived) independence from the empire but with a guarantee of Roman military assistance should they be threatened from the north.

When Antoninus decided to move the frontier north to the Clyde-Forth isthmus, he seems to have modelled his new 'wall' very much on Hadrian's (though of turf rather than stone, and without a vallum), suggesting that the latter was regarded at the time as a sound model, albeit in the wrong place. There is, of course, an argument that Hadrian should have located his wall here in the first place, from where troops could be more easily dispatched to deal with any smouldering unrest amongst the northern tribes, but as we have seen the initial concept for the Wall relied on links with existing forts along

Trajan's Stanegate frontier, so there was no real alternative. It is interesting to speculate that had the Antonine Wall not been abandoned then Hadrian's Wall would probably have been widely ridiculed, both in antiquity and in modern times, as possibly the greatest white elephant of all time. Much of its masonry would presumably have been recycled in Roman times, and Hadrian would enjoy a rather less positive press than he does currently. Fortunately (for Hadrian's reputation) the Antonine Wall, itself a colossal achievement, was abandoned after only a couple of decades and the frontier became fossilised along the line of the earlier Wall, where it remained for the final two and a half centuries of the Roman occupation. In some ways the Antonine Wall made more sense as a frontier than Hadrian's Wall, and the reasons for its abandonment are not known, though they probably related to the logistical difficulties of the extended supply line, coupled with the fact that land between the two walls seems to have been generally peaceful, thus providing an effective buffer zone between Hadrian's Wall and potentially hostile tribes in the far north with minimal need for military intervention.

The management of the Wall necessitated the continual presence of a very large garrison in the frontier region, backed up by the permanent presence of three entire legions at York, Chester and Caerleon. Hadrian's Wall differed from all other frontiers in the empire (with the brief exception of the Antonine Wall) in two particular respects: its comparatively very short length, and the great concentration of troops necessary to man it. It has been estimated that the Rhine-Danube provinces, with a frontier more than 2000km in length, beyond which lay numerous powerful potential enemies, were garrisoned by some 170,000 soldiers in the Hadrianic period. This contrasts with Britain, where as many as 50,000 men were entrusted with the defence of a frontier only 120km long, and beyond which lay nothing other than the same northern tribes that had been beaten into submission by Agricola just 34 years prior to Hadrian's accession. The explanation for this may lie largely in Britain's location across the sea; getting reinforcements here in a crisis would have been logistically much more difficult than to other sectors of the frontier. Whatever its justification, this concentration of military personnel in so small a province led to a number of known cases of military rebellions against Rome involving the commanders and men of the 'British' army, and many more smaller scale episodes may have escaped the attention of contemporary writers. It could perhaps be argued that all these problems arose from the decision to base the defence of the province on the static frontier of Hadrian's Wall. A well trained army, designed to undertake offensive field campaigns every year aimed at the acquisition of new territories from which wealth would filter indirectly back to Rome, was transformed into a static army of frontier defence. However, we should note that such problems were far from unique to Britain; military rebellions occurred in other regions of the empire, so this should not be considered a particular weakness of Hadrian's Wall.

We have seen that the Wall formed but a small portion, albeit the most architecturally impressive portion, of the frontier system extending around the entire empire. The change in what we might term 'foreign policy', from the aggressive expansionism of Trajan to consolidation under Hadrian, meant that troops no longer had to be maintained in large mobile battle groups designed to campaign beyond the frontier. Instead, the demands of frontier control necessitated smaller groups of men spread out along the edges of the empire, with concentrations at strategic points where important routeways crossed the frontiers, or at other potential weak points where enemies were thought likely to attack. In practice, the strictly military defence of the empire would perhaps have been better served had the army not become so fragmented, but the demands of Hadrian's frontier policy, which he seems to have faced little opposition in implementing, necessitated this change. The new policy, however, soon ran into serious difficulties. From the 160s and throughout the later second and third centuries, there were many invasions of the empire by Germanic and Persian armies against which the frontier appeared ineffective. Some of the earlier invasions reached deep into the heart of the empire where there was no army to repel them, necessitating the rapid redeployment of troops from the frontier, thus leaving these frontier areas under-resourced and inviting further raids. During the third century this pressure on the frontiers led to the abandonment of the province of Dacia and of land previously held to the east of the headwaters of the Rhine and Danube. Within the empire, many towns and cities, including Rome, were enclosed within new defensive walls. Within Britain, with a deep frontier zone facing a narrow frontier, backed up by three legions, the problems were not as severe as elsewhere, but in general terms the 'golden age' described by Aristides was over; the defended frontier remained in commission, but people within the empire no longer trusted it to do its job.

This constant pressure on the frontiers led to fundamental changes in the structure of the army. The detail of these changes cannot concern us here, but the Hadrianic system of legions and auxiliary units spread along the frontier was transformed into a dual system of *limitanei* (border guards stationed on the frontier and charged with everyday policing of the frontier and the interception of small-scale raids) and *comitatenses* (mobile field armies billeted in towns throughout the empire and able to travel anywhere at short notice to deal with more serious incidents, including invasions and attempted usurpations). In addition there were local provisional units known as *cunei* (cavalry) and *auxilia* (infantry - not to be confused with the earlier auxiliaries, which, along with the *numeri*, seem to have become defunct), and an elite reserve, the emperor's *scholae*. Although some units in both the border and field armies were still known as legions through into the fifth century, these bore little relation to the legions of Hadrian's time, being much smaller and far less prestigious. The border and field armies of the later empire consisted of a mix of cavalry and infantry, and included both Roman citizens and non-citizens. Also, as time went by, increasing numbers of 'barbarian' mercenaries known as *foederati* were engaged to serve alongside the *limitanei* and *comitatensis*. The new system seemed to accept that invasions would occasionally pierce the frontier, but sought to ensure that sufficient mobile resources would be available to intercept and destroy all invaders once they were on Roman soil. Despite all these changes, most frontiers, including the Wall, remained essentially where they had been under Hadrian through until the end of the fourth century; by the end of the fifth, however, they would be no more.

From the early fifth century, troops were increasingly withdrawn from frontier regions to support the mobile field army. As we saw in Chapter 2, Roman rule in Britain effectively ended in 410, the same year as Rome was sacked by the Goths under Aleric; the capital of the Western Roman Empire was now Ravenna in north-east Italy. The empire continued to shrink as more and more frontier regions were settled by invading barbarian tribes, some of which struck deep into the empire. Many groups of *foederati* rebelled, and loyal troops in some distant parts of the empire became cut off. Eventually, in 476, the Western Roman Empire was toppled. Seen from the Roman standpoint this was, of course, a great tragedy, but, let us not forget, for those who helped to topple the hated Romans it was a triumph to be celebrated with great joy, just as the Romans had themselves rejoiced a few generations earlier as they occupied region after region in their mission to conquer the world.

The fall of the Western Roman Empire is often blamed upon the later Roman army, popularly regarded as incompetent in comparison with that of the 'glory years' of the earlier empire, and Hadrian is sometimes harshly cited as the architect of the decline. Such an accusation is unfair; we saw in Chapter 1 that the army was at full stretch at the time of Hadrian's accession, giving him little choice other than to shun further expansion and consolidate the frontiers. The new structure was needed precisely because the earlier army had proved incapable of dealing with the new challenges of the late second and third centuries; had the new structure not evolved, the empire would probably have collapsed a good deal earlier than it eventually did. And of course the collapse of the empire was due to a complex web of social, cultural and economic problems; it cannot be blamed solely upon the army, and to blame it primarily on a failure of Hadrian's frontier policy, developed in response to a specific set of circumstances 350 years earlier, seems unreasonably harsh.

That said, the remains of all Roman military sites in Britain can, to an extent, be regarded as monuments to failure, as, following the collapse of Roman rule in the early fifth century, the British were left to fight new enemies and forge new kingdoms in *their* land. The archaeology of this period on the Wall, as elsewhere in Britain, is complex and, as yet, poorly understood, but it seems fair to say that neither Roman people nor Roman culture (with the single exception of the Church) would play much of a role in the subsequent development of Britain. Seen in this context, Hadrian's Wall, as the mightiest and grandest of all the military structures left behind by the Romans, can justly be regarded as *the* monument to the failure of Roman Britain. It represents the failure of the Roman Empire to conquer northern Britain, the failure of Roman Britannia to ever feel entirely secure in the face of the 'Barbarians' to the north, and, eventually, the Roman failure to hold onto what it had, as even the 'Romanised' south of England was lost. These are legitimate observations, but Hadrian himself is surely immune from blame; such problems resulted largely from varying degrees of mismanagement of the empire before and after his time.

In some ways, life may have been easier for Rome if she had simply exercised her option to conquer and occupy the whole of the island in the first place, or had never bothered to set foot in Britain at all. But there were clear benefits to Rome in the occupation of southern Britain, both in terms of industrial and agricultural production, and in the negation of the potential British threat to the coast of Gaul. In the circumstances prevailing at the time, the options of conquering Scotland or abandoning Britain were simply not available to Hadrian, who, as we have seen, enjoyed a positive relationship with his army and as far as we know never faced even a hint of military rebellion in Britain or elsewhere. His decision to consolidate the frontier and build the Wall is seen retrospectively as a good one, and it seems that the men who built it and served on it, during his reign and subsequently, may well have regarded it with a far from insubstantial degree of pride.

3b. The Wall and civilian communities

Leaving aside the Wall's ultimate origins (rooted in the failure to conquer Scotland) and final abandonment (representing the eventual failure of the province), and the few occasions on which it may have been temporarily overrun, we must conclude that it formed part of a system of frontier management that enjoyed considerable success over three centuries. During this time, many changes occurred in the relationships between the army and the local population. At the onset of Roman rule in northern England, nearly half a century before the commencement of work on the Wall, local attitudes to Rome are not recorded but would presumably have been mixed. Perhaps they mirrored, to an extent, the views of early 21st-century tribal groups in Afghanistan or Iraq towards western forces; some people saw sense in siding with the occupying forces, while others would do anything, including sacrificing their lives, to rid their homeland of the foreign 'aggressors'. Such attitudes may have varied, even within individual tribes or families, but the initial effect of the Wall on the local population must have been dramatic. Recent air photographic surveys suggest the Wall was built in a busy landscape, with much evidence for contemporary settlement and agriculture. This evidence (though currently lacking accurate dating due to the lack of recent excavations) suggests that the Wall may never have existed, as traditionally assumed, in an unpopulated 'military zone'. As noted above, we do not know the extent to which local people may have supported or opposed the construction of the Wall, but by the 'end' of the Wall, a dozen or so generations later, distinctions between 'Roman' and 'native' would inevitably have become blurred. Some 'British' families would, no doubt, be able to point to generations of military service in the 'Roman' army, and it is interesting to speculate as to the extent that Brigantian or Votadinian individuals may have considered themselves Roman. Perhaps the situation was not dissimilar to that of many people in the same region today, who may consider themselves primarily Northumbrian, English, British or European. Certainly there must have been a blurring of boundaries, as is suggested by recent DNA studies claiming to demonstrate that a million or more present-day British men are direct descendents of Roman military personnel.

It is important when seeking to assess the significance of the Wall to consider the wider landscape, not to focus on Roman military sites in isolation. Although little is known for certain, and much new fieldwork is required to improve our understanding of the landscape throughout the Roman occupation, some intriguing patterns can perhaps be tantalisingly glimpsed from the currently available data. 'Vici' (civilian settlements) grew up at several forts along the Wall, providing a range of services to the serving soldiers. The people who lived in these settlements presumably included many who moved here from surrounding farmsteads and villages, perhaps spending some of their time working in the vici and some back 'home' in what we like to call 'native settlements'. Whatever the arrangements, there was clearly much interaction between the 'native' and 'Roman' worlds throughout the Wall corridor. It seems that the vici thrived until the mid third century, after which they declined; the reasons of this decline are not known, though it may relate in some way to changes in the fort garrisons. Substantial urban centres grew up at Carlisle and Corbridge, where the main roads northwards crossed the frontier, and these flourished during the fourth century after the vici had gone into irreversible decline. Whatever the detailed chronology, the presence of urban centres and vici immediately south of the Wall would seem to suggest that the Wall itself did meet with some success in demarcating a zone of 'Romanisation' to its south, within which people lived 'Roman lives' within the towns and vici, while things were different to the north. This may be taken as evidence that Hadrian's stated objective of building a wall between 'Roman' and 'barbarian' met with considerable success, creating a pattern that survived for three centuries through until the end of Roman Britain.

This idea also receives support from an analysis of rural settlement to either side of the Wall. Again, we must base our generalisations on a paucity of data from a handful of sites, but a fascinating pattern does seem to be emerging. To the north of the Wall, many native settlements seem to have been abandoned during the second century. The reasons for this are unclear, but they may well relate in some way to the construction of the Wall in the 120s. In complete contrast, on the south side of the Wall, probable villas have now been recorded as far north as County Durham, just 20km from the Wall. The recent recognition of a small 'town' at Hardwick Park (Sedgefield) in County Durham provides further evidence of Romanisation of the landscape here during the second century. Clearly, more fieldwork is needed, but it really does begin to appear as though the Wall may have functioned as a limit to Roman-isation, with towns, vici and villas to the south, and a wholesale reorganisation of the landscape to the north. The extent to which this may have been by Roman decree, or simply a result of increasing numbers of people opting to move south and 'become Roman', is not known, but this is a fascinating field that demands further study, like so many aspects of the complex relationships between 'Romans' and 'natives' throughout the occupation.

Although the two are very different, comparisons are sometimes drawn between Hadrian's Wall and the Berlin Wall; the latter being something that only lasted three decades but which people from both sides could not tear down fast enough once the opportunity arose. Both walls were imposed on the landscape and on the population by military dictatorships in an attempt to control the movements of people and the development of ideologies, but they were also very different. The Berlin Wall was constructed (at least from a western perspective) primarily to keep people in and western or capitalist ideas out, in order to enable the promotion of 'socialist' ideology. Hadrian's Wall, as suggested above, was probably intended to keep potential enemies out, while enabling the encouragement of Romanisation 'within'. Of course, the argument could be made that the builders of the Berlin Wall saw it as essential to the encouragement of socialist ideology within East Berlin, just as Hadrian's Wall was a tool to encourage 'Romanisation' within Britannia, but in terms of controlling the movement of people it is usually assumed that more were trying to 'escape from' rather than 'break into' East Berlin, whereas the opposite is generally assumed to have been the case for Hadrian's Wall and Roman territory.

Another difference lies in the grandeur of the architectural styles of the two walls: the Berlin Wall, although it became hugely symbolic, was built rapidly, and cheaply, as a functional barrier, whereas it has been argued above that Hadrian's Wall, with its awe-inspiring architecture (even allowing for the realisation that some of its workmanship was rather less grand than it could have been), was, from its inception, as much a symbolic as a practical structure. The Berlin Wall was hated by people on both sides of it, but while in commission, was undeniably effective: quite possibly more effective than Hadrian's Wall ever was at controlling the passage of determined individuals or small groups. Today, regardless of the operational effectiveness of either Wall, Hadrian enjoys an enviable reputation throughout the world, while the same cannot be said of those who supervised the construction of the Berlin Wall. It is quite possible that Hadrian had his long-term reputation very much in mind when ordering the construction of his Wall. Certainly, such matters would have concerned him more than the comparative inconsequence of a few people sneaking across the barrier from time to time. It could be argued that, while it was properly manned, Hadrian's Wall exercised its control through its sheer *demonstration* of power: there was simply no need for Rome to concern herself about occasional individuals seeking to cross it in a fashion akin to the desperate and horrific attempts to cross the Berlin Wall that were occasionally caught so dramatically on camera. It is also important to realise that the Berlin Wall existed in relative isolation, whereas Hadrian's Wall was only one element of a frontier zone, with troops garrisoned to north and south. The extent to which the actual fabric of Hadrian's Wall made any difference to the defence of the province must be open to much doubt.

Regardless of the views of the immediate local population (and these were probably never uniform, and must have fluctuated over time), it would seem that communities much further to the north remained resolutely opposed to Rome. These people may have regarded the Wall as a hated symbol of imperialist aggression, to be pierced at every available opportunity. As such, the Wall may have actively promoted anti-Roman sentiment, and, on the occasions that the province was sacked by marauding northern tribes, the actual passage through the Wall, both on the way south and subsequently on the way back home, must have been moments of great symbolic significance. Such events, however, seem to have been few and far between, having little or no long-term impact on the Wall, which, in addition to its practical value, presumably retained considerable symbolic value for Rome.

We may, therefore, conclude that the Wall appears to have met with some success in controlling the activities of the native people in what is now northern England and southern Scotland, but perhaps had little effect on those further north, for whom it may well have acted as a magnet, drawing them south to plunder the province whenever the opportunity arose. Such people were not interested in capturing Roman territory, but simply in sacking and looting the province before returning home with as much booty as they could carry. Indeed, it has reasonably been argued that frontiers such as Hadrian's, with economic development encouraged behind them leading to much greater prosperity immediately inside the frontier than outside, contain the seeds of their own destruction as those 'without' are tempted to try and help themselves to some of the wealth 'within'. Perhaps the Romans would have fared better had they sought to 'control' the northern natives by direct military force or political negotiation, rather than by constructing an outwardly aggressive looking monument for primarily defensive purposes. In Roman eyes the Wall may have stood as a powerful symbol of the mighty empire, but in the eyes of successive northern tribal leaders it stood as an open invitation, and a challenge, to sack the hated imperial province to the south.

Archaeologists are in general agreement that one of the original aims of Hadrian's Wall was to help exercise control over the natives. I cannot help but wonder what the Romans would have thought if they could see the extent to which the ruins of their old wall still control the activities of the natives today! Hadrian, I have no doubt, would be most amused. These ruins, through local, national and international regulations and guidelines, exercise control over everything to do with the landscape, including the location and form of new buildings, the nature of agricultural practices, the location of industrial activity and of woodland. These controls extend far beyond the stones and mortar of the Wall itself, so much so that a decision relating to a new quarry or a wind farm several miles from the Wall might be determined by its potential impact on the views to be enjoyed from the line of the Wall. This is because Hadrian's Wall is now a World Heritage Site, demanding strict conservation policies which necessitate much control over the activities of the people who live and work in the area.

Given that the Wall was (and still is) so much about controlling people, some may think it appropriate that Tynedale District Council (the local planning authority for a large proportion of the Wall corridor prior to local government reorganisation in 2009) used a Hadrianic coin as the basis for its official logo. One wonders whether the individuals responsible for adopting this logo cared about, or were even interested in, the fact that Hadrian was 'universally loathed when he died'. Although some may consider a loathsome figure an appropriate public face for a planning authority, the intention was presumably to link the council with Hadrian on more positive economic and marketing grounds. Our tendency to regard Hadrian as a great man, seen in the naming of dozens of local institutions and businesses (including schools, hotels, travel agents, vets, dentists, butchers, sandwich makers, take-aways and numerous others) would appear very strange to any natives who opposed Rome back in the first and second centuries, many of whom lost their lives confronting the hated 'imperial aggressor'. It might legitimately be compared to the unlikely future scenarios of the Tibetans glorifying the Chinese, the Poles celebrating Nazi occupation, or the Palestinians praising the creation of Israel. This strange worshipping of all things Roman owes much, albeit subconsciously, to the nature of British imperialism. But whatever its explanation, and despite the eventual failure of Roman Britain, it is clear that Hadrian has won the long-term battle in the popularity stakes. Today, his shortcomings are generally glossed over, and his Wall is seen by pretty much everyone as a great monument to his foresight in consolidating the boundaries of the empire. He may well have had such a long-term view in mind when designing the Wall, but if so has surely exceeded even his own high expectations. We should note here that this 'Hadrian's Wall phenomenon' extends far beyond the local landscape, perhaps most intriguingly to Hadrian Manufacturing Inc, 'North America's leading toilet partition and locker manufacturer', whose website notes that Hadrian's Wall provides the inspiration for the company's name and its 'creative, high quality and desirable products', adding that 'perhaps Publius Aelius Hadrianus, the great emperor himself, would be pleased with the modern day association.'

Finally in this section, we should briefly acknowledge that some people come to Hadrian's Wall country for reasons other than archaeology: perhaps to seek the solitude, peace and quiet depicted in the tourist brochures but increasingly hard to find on the ground; to experience the beautiful scenery; or to get themselves photographed beneath 'Kevin Costner's tree' at Sycamore Gap, bizarrely now a major attraction in its own right following its role in the 1991 film *Robin Hood: Prince of Thieves*. Such people may not wish to know anything about Romans, and there is nothing wrong with that. However, there is no doubt that Hadrian, through the ruins of his Wall, will continue to play a key role in the management of this landscape, and native communities in Hadrian's Wall Country will continue to feel his influence in the centuries and millennia to come.

Summary
Hadrian's Wall - alternative interpretations

If you ask two archaeologists the same question, you will, more often than not, get at least three answers. This is because archaeology involves not only the acquisition of 'facts' about the past, but also the interpretation of often ambiguous 'evidence'. The facts can in themselves be interesting, but interpreting them to tell meaningful stories about how people may have lived in the past can be much more fascinating, if sometimes also rather frustrating. This is certainly true with regard to Hadrian and his Wall.

The basic design of the Wall as originally planned is essentially very simple, and the 'revised' plan with forts and vallum, although less straightforward is still far from complex. Many aspects of the Wall's interpretation today are, however, far from simple. If this book has demonstrated anything, it is surely that the conventional view of the Wall as a barrier against northern 'barbarians' is rather simplistic and certainly open to question. It will have come as a surprise to many readers that we don't even know what the Wall looked like, or precisely when it was built, never mind why it was built, or how it was meant to function. It is reasonable to assume that the Wall's three main purposes were those discussed in the preceding sections, namely frontier control, military defence and what we might term 'Roman rhetoric'. It is legitimate to question the extent to which each of these may have been uppermost in Hadrian's mind, the minds of those engaged in the construction of the Wall, and the minds of all those who experienced it during its three centuries of active service. We could suggest perhaps 20% defence, 30% customs barrier, and 50% rhetoric, but to attempt such a calculation, focussing on one supposed purpose at the expense of the others, misses the whole point of the project. I believe the Wall was conceived from the outset as a multipurpose monument; the three 'alternative purposes' were not viewed as alternatives, rather they merged with each other in Hadrian's mind, and are thus represented together in the fabric of the Wall. The Wall may have been over-engineered in terms of its everyday functions, but it was a thoroughly brilliant concept, designed from the start to merge rhetoric with practical frontier management. Such a view sees the Wall as a magnificent multi-purpose architectural masterpiece, built by a caring emperor who sought peace on the boundaries of his empire, and who regarded the Wall's construction as a unifying force for his troops who would be engaged on an architectural project to the glory of Rome; glory that had previously been achievable only through military conquest.

That said, it is possible to interpret the Wall as a poorly built structure, so inappropriately designed that the plans had to be radically amended while work was in progress, imposed on the landscape (and arguably built in the wrong place) by a megalomaniac emperor keen to stamp his personal mark on the northern edge of his empire, and ultimately irrelevant to the defence of the province when seaborne invaders arrived on the east coast in the early fifth century. Thus, the Wall can be seen, on the one hand, as primarily a monument to failure, an absurd over-reaction to a perceived threat from the north and only necessary because Rome had failed to conquer the north of the island, or, on the other, as the major installation in a very successful frontier system that encouraged Romanisation to its south and helped to keep the peace for nearly three centuries, being overrun on just a few occasions when perhaps its garrison had been reduced in the face of priorities elsewhere. Future work will certainly provide more 'facts' about the form and chronology of the Wall, and these will be used to develop new interpretations, some of which may acknowledge Hadrian as a genius while others might paint him in less favourable light. Either way, the Wall remains a magnificent spectacle, and a wholly appropriate monument to the man who dreamt it up.

Objects such as the Staffordshire Pan suggest that Hadrian's Wall was regarded in its own time as something special, but we must not lose sight of the fact that it was not built as a World Heritage Site for the amusement of tourists. It was built by a brutally efficient military force as part of the attempt to consolidate a troublesome corner of a vast empire. Once constructed, an enormous static garrison was required to hold it, which in itself led to serious political problems on several occasions. It was apparently breached several times by 'barbarians'. Today, its atmospheric ruins say as much about the failure of the Roman Empire as they do about its temporary triumphs. It could be considered a failure on a number of grounds, and these should be reflected in its modern day interpretation. However, if Hadrian's main aim in building the wall was self-aggrandisement then it must be considered an unqualified success; success reflected in the fact that you are currently reading about him nearly two millennia after he breathed his last breath. He would have rather liked the idea of the Wall being a World Heritage Site, studied by schoolchildren in distant lands of which he himself was wholly unaware in his lifetime, and he would have been amused that the main threat to the well-being of what is left of his Wall comes not in the form of hordes of wild northern savages, but through erosion generated by tourists from all around the world, increasing numbers of whom now descend on this beautiful landscape each year to walk the Hadrian's Wall Path National Trail, opened in 2003 and itself in constant need of specialist maintenance.

A further thing to consider, when seeking to interpret the Wall, is that we should be wary of falling into the cunning psychological trap set for us by Hadrian through his architectural projects. This trap uses the power of architecture, in this case the astonishing scale of the Wall complex, linked to the strength of the forces that built and manned it, to ensnare us, almost subconsciously, into regarding the Roman Empire with awe – to look up to the Roman way of life as somehow superior in every way to that of the sorry 'barbarian'. The Roman way of life was certainly different to that of the native Iron Age, but whether or not it was really so much 'better' is certainly open to question. Many regions that were never conquered by Rome have coped quite satisfactorily over the past two millennia, and many people today regard the heritage of the Celtic fringe or Scandinavian nations, with their lack of Roman influence, as spiritually rather richer than that of England.

This book has not paid as much attention as it could (and probably should) have done to other Roman frontiers, but it is probably fair to say that these seem to have been more about controlling the everyday passage of people into and out of the empire, and the discouragement of small-scale cross-border raids, than the interception and annihilation of invading armies. As we have seen, the architecture of Hadrian's Wall makes more sense in this context than if we try to interpret it primarily as a military barrier. It is legitimate to ask why other artificial frontier barriers were not afforded a comparable degree of architectural extravagance; the explanation is not immediately obvious, but must surely be in large part due to Hadrian's personal desire to do something special here.

Potentially comparable barriers from the modern world, of which Berlin, Belfast, the West Bank, and the Mexico/USA border provide the best-known examples, are all about controlling (in the most part preventing) the passage of individuals or small groups of people, not the repelling of large-scale military invasions. We have to admit, however, that none of these examples is directly comparable with Hadrian's Wall. All are individual responses to particular sets of circumstances, just as was the Wall. Although rarely commented upon, the Maginot line, a 25km deep system of fortifications constructed by the French military at vast expense in the 1930s to deter a surprise German attack, and in the event of such an attack to buy time for the mobilisation and deployment of French forces, perhaps offers, in some ways, a more viable comparison. The Maginot Line was solely about deterring an invasion, and of course it failed dismally as the Germans simply bypassed it; a fate that would have been impossible for Hadrian's Wall other than by seaborne invaders, which is, of course, exactly what happened in the early fifth century as invaders sailed across the North Sea.

From the ancient world, the Great Wall of China, parts of which date originally from the third century BC, provides another potentially relevant comparison. Indeed, it is quite possible that Hadrian was aware of this great wall, built in a distant land to keep out northern invaders, and that it provided some of the inspiration for his own project. The Wall of China was consolidated and extended on many occasions through into medieval times, and what we see of it in today's tourist brochures is much later in date than Hadrian's Wall. This doesn't necessarily render comparisons irrelevant, however, and much fascinating work could probably be done comparing aspects of Roman frontiers and the Great Wall.

Years ago, I used to delight in giving a deliberately controversial, but in my view perfectly fair, public lecture entitled *Hadrian's Wall – Monument to Failure*. This focussed on the negative interpretations noted above, and invariably proved popular with general audiences who had never previously heard the Wall discussed in such a way. Such views are often glossed over in books about the Wall that tend to be written by Roman specialists, schooled in the glories of Rome and often paying little heed to the complex lives that non-Roman communities lived in places like northern England and Scotland. These conventional interpretations are rooted in the days of British imperialism, when both the British (or should that be English?) and Roman Empires were regarded as forces for good, spreading civilisation amongst uneducated 'native' populations. My lecture sought to stress that the Wall was experienced by both Romans and non-Romans, and the views of the latter should be as relevant to our interpretations of it as those of the former. Any comprehensive interpretation of the Wall must consider the ways in which it was seen by Caledonian tribesmen, or Brigantian farmers across whose fields it was driven, and how these views may have changed through time, as well as the views of Roman emperors, generals, and humble auxiliary soldiers. Much stimulating work remains to be done in this field.

As I have studied Hadrian's Wall over recent years, I have come to regard it rather less as a 'monument to failure' and more as the magnificent response of an extraordinary man to a unique set of circumstances; Hadrian cannot be held responsible for Rome's failure to conquer the whole of Britain prior to his reign, or for events following his death. As the experimental nature of much of his architecture demonstrates, he was always prepared to modify plans to take account of changing circumstances, and he would certainly have expected those who followed him to be flexible with regard to frontier arrangements in the face of new challenges. Personally, I suspect that his motivation for building the Wall was essentially commendable and that he genuinely saw it as of benefit to the province and therefore to the empire. However, he was also well aware that future generations would credit him personally with its construction, and this would have been a far from minor consideration in his mind. In later life, he may have had little interest in it, and probably did not consider it amongst his greatest architectural achievements, but today it ensures that his name ranks amongst the most famous in the whole of human history. Through the building of several magnificent structures, but most notably his Wall, Hadrian was truly the architect of his own immortality.

Further Reading

Several books have been published about Hadrian, and many about his Wall, but surprisingly few that consider both in any detail. Readers that wish to explore either subject in further detail are encouraged to consult the following volumes, which in turn contain many references to primary sources such as detailed excavation reports and original classical texts.

Those marked with asterisks are particularly good introductions for readers wishing to explore Hadrian and/or his Wall in greater detail.

On Hadrian.

*Birley, A.R. 1997. *Hadrian: the Restless Emperor.* London & New York: Routledge.

Boatwright, M.T. 1987. *Hadrian and the City of Rome.* Princeton & Oxford: Princeton University Press.

Boatwright, M.T. 2000. *Hadrian and the Cities of the Roman Empire.* Princeton & Oxford: Princeton University Press.

Danziger, D. & Purcell, N. 2005. *Hadrian's Empire. When Rome Ruled the World.* London: Hodder & Stoughton.

English Heritage. 2010. *An Archaeological Map of Hadrian's Wall (1:25,000 scale).* London: English Heritage.

Everitt, A. 2009. *Hadrian and the Triumph of Rome.* New York: Random House.

Lambert, R. 1984. *Beloved and God. The Story of Hadrian and Antinous.* London: Weidenfeld & Nicolson.

MacDonald, W.L. & Pinto, J.A. 1995. *Hadrian's Villa and Its Legacy.* New Haven & London: Yale University Press.

*Opper, T. 2008. *Hadrian. Empire and Conflict.* London: British Museum Press.

Perowne, S. H. 1960. *Hadrian.* London: Hodder & Stoughton.

Rathbone D. (ed). 2008. *Lives of Hadrian from Cassius Dio and The Historia Augusta.* London: Pallas Athene.

Speller, E. 2002. *Following Hadrian. A Second-century Journey through the Roman Empire.* London: Review.

Yourcenar, M. 1954. *Memoirs of Hadrian.* London: Secker & Warburg.
(In contrast to the above historical works, this is perhaps best described as a 'ghosted autobiography' – a brilliant attempt, using all available historical and archaeological sources, to 'recreate' Hadrian's lost autobiography. Originally published in French in 1951, it is a wonderful book and represents essential reading for anyone seeking an understanding of Hadrian's character).

On Hadrian's Wall and other Roman frontiers.

Bidwell, P. (ed). 2008. *Understanding Hadrian's Wall*. South Shields: The Arbeia Society.

*Breeze, D.J. 2006. *J. Collingwood Bruce's Handbook to the Roman Wall* (14th edition). Newcastle upon Tyne: Society of Antiquaries of Newcastle upon Tyne.

Breeze, D.J. 2007. *Roman Frontiers in Britain*. London: Bristol Classical Press.

Breeze, D.J. 2011. *Frontiers of the Roman Empire*. Barnsley: Pen & Sword.

*Breeze, D.J. & Dobson, B. 2000. *Hadrian's Wall* (4th edition). London: Penguin.

Bruce, J. C. 1867. *The Roman Wall. A Description of the Mural Barrier of the North of England.* (Third edition). London: Longmans, Green, Reader & Dyer. Newcastle upon Tyne: Andrew Reid.

de la Bedoyere, G. 1998. *Hadrian's Wall. History & Guide.* Stroud: Tempus.

Elston, H. 1996. *Frontiers of the Roman Empire*. London: Batsford.

Ewin, A. 2000. *Hadrian's Wall. A Social and Cultural History.* Lancaster: Centre for North-West Regional Studies, University of Lancaster.

Hill, P. 2006. *The Construction of Hadrian's Wall*. Tempus: Stroud.

Hodgson, N. (ed). 2009. *Hadrian's Wall 1999-2009. A Summary of Excavation and Research prepared for The Thirteenth Pilgrimage of Hadrian's Wall, 8-14 August 2009.* Kendal: Cumberland and Westmorland Antiquarian and Archaeological Society/The Society of Antiquaries of Newcastle upon Tyne.

Johnson, S. 1989. *Hadrian's Wall*. London: Batsford/English Heritage.

Jones, G.D.B. & Woolliscroft, D.J. 2001. *Hadrian's Wall from the air*. Stroud: Tempus.

Parker, P. 2009. *The Empire Stops Here. A Journey along the Frontiers of the Roman World.* London: Jonathan Cape.

Poulter, J. 2010. *The Planning of Roman Roads and Walls in Northern Britain*. Stroud: Amberley.

Shotter, D. 1996. *The Roman Frontier in Britain*. Preston: Carnegie.

Symonds, M.F.A. & Mason, D.J.P. Undated (2009). *Frontiers of Knowledge. A Research Framework for Hadrian's Wall, Part of the Frontiers of the Roman Empire World Heritage Site.* Durham University/Durham County Council/English Heritage.

Wilmott, T. (ed). 2009. *Hadrian's Wall: Archaeological Research by English Heritage, 1976 – 2000.* London: English Heritage.

Woodside, R. & Crow, J. 1999. *Hadrian's Wall. An Historic Landscape.* The National Trust.

Academic Papers

Numerous academic papers have been published in various journals dealing with all manner of subjects relating to the Wall, many of which are referenced within the bibliographies of the above books. Listed here are just five such papers, all published in *Archaeologia Aeliana* (the distinguished journal of the Society of Antiquaries of Newcastle upon Tyne, named after *Pons Aelius*, in turn, of course, named after Hadrian). All are essential reading for anyone seeking a better understanding of Hadrian and his Wall.

Breeze, D.J. 2009. **Did Hadrian Design Hadrian's Wall?** *Archaeologia Aeliana* 5th series, vol 38, p87-103.

Dobson, B. 1986. **The Function of Hadrian's Wall.** *Archaeologia Aeliana* 5th series, vol 14, p5-30.

Graafstal, E. P. 2012. **Hadrian's haste: a priority programme for the Wall.** *Archaeologia Aeliana* 5th Series, Vol 41, p123-184

Mann, J.C. 1990. **The Function of Hadrian's Wall.** *Archaeologia Aeliana* 5th series, vol 18, p51-54.

Maxfield, V.A. 1990. **Hadrian's Wall in its Imperial Setting.** *Archaeologia Aeliana* 5th series, vol 18, p1-27.

Visiting Hadrian's Wall

By Nigel Mills. World Heritage & Access Director, The Hadrian's Wall Trust.

There is no better way to understand Hadrian's Wall than by visiting it and exploring some of the stories and issues yourself! Much of the remaining Wall and many of its milecastles and turrets can be visited free of charge. Several of the Wall forts are also open to the public but there is usually a charge. These forts are managed by a number of different organisations: Arbeia and Segedunum – Tyne and Wear Archives and Museums; Chesters and Birdoswald – English Heritage; Housesteads – English Heritage and the National Trust; Vindolanda – The Vindolanda Trust;

The Great North Museum in Newcastle and the Roman Frontier Gallery at Tullie House Museum and Art Gallery in Carlisle provide visitors with an overview of the whole story of Hadrian's Wall. The Great North Museum contains a superb collection of sculpture and inscriptions from across the Wall and the displays focus on the Wall itself. The Roman Frontier Gallery explores the wider story of Rome's north west frontier, both before and after Hadrian including the various advances into Scotland and the Antonine Wall. The displays also explore the impact of the Roman occupation on Britain. Other museums to visit are the Roman Army Museum at Carvoran, the Senhouse Museum at Maryport and the Corbridge Museum and Roman site.

One of the best areas to visit to gain an impression of the Wall and its associated structures is the five mile stretch in Cumbria between Banks and Gilsland including the fort at Birdoswald. Along this stretch you find well preserved turrets and milecastles (including perhaps the best preserved milecastle at Poltross Burn in Gilsland), a fragment of the turf wall, parts of the vallum, the well preserved fort at Birdoswald itself, abutments for the bridge across the Irthing river, and perhaps the best preserved and longest sections of the Wall itself just to the east of the fort.

The central section between Walltown Quarry and Limestone Corner requires more demanding walking as the dramatic landscape has many sharp up and downs and is some distance from the road. As well as the forts at Housesteads and Vindolanda there are many fine stretches of the Wall here as well as turrets and milecastles.

There is much to see also in the urban area of Newcastle. The vallum crossing at Benwell gives a fascinating insight into the scale and significance of this striking and enigmatic structure. The reconstructions of Roman buildings at Arbeia and at Segedunum give a real sense of the scale and sophistication of Roman architecture. Across the road from the fort at Segedunum there is a fine reconstructed length of the Wall beside an excavated section of the Wall itself where you can also see the remains of *cippi*.

Both Carlisle and Newcastle are good bases from which to explore the Wall with the Frontier Gallery (Carlisle) and the Great North Museum (Newcastle) providing contrasting overviews of the whole story. From here you can access the main parts of the Wall by car or using public transport. The Hadrian's Wall Country railway line between Carlisle and Newcastle connects with the AD 122 Hadrian's Wall Bus service (Easter to October) at Hexham and Haltwhistle.

For walkers, the Hadrian's Wall Path National Trail runs the whole length from Bowness on Solway to Wallsend. Add a couple of extra days to allow time to visit the sites along the way! There are also many shorter routes suitable for walkers of all abilities which enable visitors to explore many different aspects of Hadrian and his Wall across Hadrian's Wall Country. For cyclists there is the Hadrian's Cycleway that allows you to explore the various sites along the Cumbria coast as well.

Hadrian's Wall is part of the Frontiers of the Roman Empire World Heritage Site which currently includes the Antonine Wall in Scotland and the Upper German/Raetian Limes in Germany. Hadrian's Wall is a Scheduled Ancient Monument. The monument needs constant management and maintenance to protect and conserve it from erosion and deterioration caused by time, weather, climate change and the tramp of hundreds of thousands of visitors' feet. In the nineteenth century John Clayton recognised these problems and did much to repair and consolidate some of the most iconic stretches of the Wall in Northumberland. These sections of the Wall now need repair along with other less well-known and evident parts of the monument that are even more at risk. The SITA Trust Heritage Fund has provided funding to help repair and consolidate these iconic stretches of Hadrian's Wall, supported by contributions from the National Trust and public donations contributed through the Co-operative Group.

The Hadrian's Wall Trust

Hadrian's Wall is a UNESCO World Heritage Site. The monitoring, conservation and protection of the World Heritage Site and the provision of access and information to visitors to enable them to enjoy it is very costly.

The Hadrian's Wall Trust is a charity whose objectives are to co-ordinate and to promote:
- the protection and management of the Hadrian's Wall World Heritage Site,
- public understanding of the World Heritage Site including education, research and lifelong learning
- sustainable development associated with the World Heritage Site to provide social and economic benefits to local communities and businesses

The Trust's role is to co-ordinate and lead all aspects of managing the Hadrian's Wall World Heritage Site for the long term benefit of local communities, working in partnership with a wide range of partners and stakeholders. The Trust is dependent on raising money through charitable donations, philanthropy, sponsorship, projects and other means to fund this important work to ensure Hadrian's Wall is protected and enjoyed for future generations. Visit our website at **www.visithadrianswall.co.uk** to find out how you can help us.

Further information.

For up to date information on the World Heritage Site, places to visit, itineraries, opening times, bus and rail timetables, information for walkers and cyclists, how to help protect and conserve Hadrian's Wall and much more visit the Hadrian's Wall Country and World Heritage Site website at:

www.visithadrianswall.co.uk

For detailed information about particular sites and parts of Hadrian's Wall, visit the following websites:

www.vindolanda.com/Vindolanda-Trust *(Vindolanda and the Roman Army Museum)*

www.english-heritage.org.uk *(Birdoswald, Housesteads, Chesters, Corbridge)*

www.nationaltrust.org.uk *(Housesteads area)*

www.northumberlandnationalpark.org.uk *(Hadrian's Wall and landscapes in the central section of the World Heritage Site)*

www.tulliehouse.co.uk *(The Roman Frontier Gallery and the Tullie House Museum and Art Gallery)*

www.twmuseums.org.uk *(Arbeia, Segedunum and the Great North Museum)*

www.senhousemuseum.co.uk *(The Senhouse collection at Maryport)*

Index

This index uses Anglicised versions of personal names (eg Hadrian, Marcus Aurelius, Trajan) where these are in general use. Other Latin names are indexed by *nomen* or family name (eg Aelius Hadrianus Afer, Publius; Hadrian's father).

Places along Hadrian's Wall are generally indexed by their English names, with Latin names in brackets where appropriate; Vindolanda, now universally known by its Latin name, is a notable exception. This index does not include references to illustrations, which are on unnumbered pages.